Artist

Cover art and above, *Cueva de las Manos* (The Cave of Hands)

The very first artists were ancestors who stenciled their hands on the walls of prehistoric caves around the globe. The finest examples can be found in Cueva de las Manos (The Cave of Hands) in Argentine Patagonia. The oldest of these hands was discovered in the Maltravieso cave in Cáceres, Spain, and is thought to be some 64,000 years old. From Argentina and Spain to France, Australia, Indonesia, and even the United States, the discovery of these hands on walls has made us wonder about the role of artists in human evolution.

What People Are Saying about *Artist*

"From the perspective of a Hollywood studio executive, I am blown away by the wisdom and heart legendary acting teacher Jocelyn Jones imparts in her book, *Artist*. More than a how-to on becoming a great actor, *Artist* is a roadmap of how to become a brilliant human being. This book is as thrilling and inspiring as Steven Pressfield's classic, *The War of Art*, and should be a staple in any class encouraging creativity and imagination. I only wish I'd read this early in my career; I would have been wiser and more understanding. I encourage everyone interested in enriching their life and craft to read this book."

—DAVID PAUL KIRKPATRICK, former President of Paramount Pictures, former Production Chief of Walt Disney Studios

"*Artist* is the definitive look at the life and creation of the artist within you. Being an artist is a daily practice, and this book gives you the tools to embrace that life. It is a beautiful tribute to the soul of the artist and their creative process. Take the Journey with Jocelyn Jones. It's worth it!"

—MICHAEL PRESSMAN, producer, director, writer, winner of two Primetime Emmys

"Let me just say this—I feel the same excitement and enthusiasm as when I read *The Artist's Way* over thirty years ago. Jocelyn Jones' *Artist* is elevating—as if channeled through an ascended master while grounded with a best friend."

—DAVID KNOLLER, producer, director, winner of a Critics Choice Award, an AFI Award, three NAACP Image Awards, and two Primetime Emmys

"Having studied with Jocelyn, I can tell you: I've never met anyone who loves artists the way she does. Jocelyn saw me. The real me! The artist beneath all my pain and protection. She saw my heart and opened me up to it. She is one of my most treasured friends, and through reading this book, she'll become one of yours, too. *Artist* will open your heart and lead you to the artist inside. Enjoy the journey!"

—LEAH REMINI, actress, writer, producer, winner of two Primetime Emmys, and a PGA Award

"I absolutely love this book! Jocelyn Jones takes us on a spiritual journey that educates, inspires, and revitalizes the artist within. Her lessons and techniques are invaluable both professionally and personally. Being a student of Jocelyn's for over twenty years, it was a pleasure to gain insight into all that shaped her into the loving, caring artist and teacher she is today. As a reader, you'll want to put her lessons into action immediately. *Artist* is a gift to your body, mind, and soul! It will lead you to your authentic self—the artist within."

—LANA PARRILLA, actress, director, winner of two TV Guide Awards, a Teen Choice Award winner, and an ALMA Award

"Staggering! Jocelyn Jones inspires us all with her wisdom, spirit, artistry, and life!"

"As a teacher of both acting and living, Jocelyn's guidance has influenced almost every aspect of my life. She's like an angel lighting the way. I am blessed to have been her student and so happy she is sharing this book with us. *Artist* is a gift!"

"This book is amazing! In sharing her life's journey, Jocelyn makes us acutely aware of our own unique gifts. She offers invaluable tools. Tools that help us realize we have the ability to manifest everything we want. Tools that help us live in the NOW. Tools that help us realize how fulfilled we are when we truly live our lives in gratitude. I love, love, love this book."

Artist

AWAKENING
THE SPIRIT WITHIN

JOCELYN JONES

GOODSPEED
P R E S S

COPYRIGHT © 2022 JOCELYN JONES

ARTIST

Awakening the Spirit Within

ISBN   978-1-5445-2830-4   *Hardcover*

978-1-5445-2829-8   *Paperback*

978-1-5445-2831-1   *Ebook*

978-1-5445-2832-8   *Audiobook*

This book is dedicated to my three greatest loves:

My husband, Miles

My daughter, Samantha

And to the trees, who raised me…

Contents

Artist

The artist is a soulful sort of being

*A person who longs to express their experience
in some way*

They leave behind a trail of breadcrumbs

Like colored hands on cave walls

Reaching back to the age of stone

"I am here! I am alive!

My hand, therefore, I am!"

Once you see those hands on walls

Calling out as if to say hello

From there to here

From you to me

And back to you again

You are forever transformed

As if awakened to the timelessness that is NOW

All those hands

Reaching out through the ether

Somebody saw it

Somebody dreamed the idea

And once it was thought, it was done

And once it was done, it belonged to everyone

The artist sees what no one has seen before

And once expressed is embraced by all

As if it had always been there

At their most inspired, the artist seeks not only to express the truth of their discoveries but also to point us in the direction of our better angels. Their mission in life is to remind us that the potential of humanity is immeasurable.

The artist seeks to discover what we can *be* beyond what we already are.

Introduction

"Inside you there's an artist you don't know about."

—RUMI

This book is not your usual memoir

It is a teacher's tale

The stories told hold the seeds to personal lessons

The lessons learned grew into a teaching

The teaching bore more seeds

And on it goes

I offer this book to you because you are seeking

And because you found it

Or maybe because it found you

I am a teacher first and foremost. A reluctant teacher, true. One who—as you will learn—found traditional education insufferable. One who instead offers tools that inspire others to discover for themselves.

I believe there is an artist in everyone, and connecting to that creative source will lead you to your heart's desire.

I believe the evolution of humanity is the art of consciousness becoming aware of itself.

I believe we are far more than a person—we are a presence. And that presence of awareness is available to guide us in our life and art.

Asleep on the Job

We live in turbulent times, distracted by the complications of artificial intelligence, algorithms, and an ever-present tsunami of advertising and "influencers" coming at us from every direction.

We are bombarded with "information" from an out-of-control media hell-bent on telling us what we should think. How we should feel. What we should look like. How much to buy. Who we must vote for. And what and whom we should hate.

We are exhausted by a pandemic. Terrified by our political landscape. Overwhelmed by the environmental crisis. And despondent at man's inhumanity to man. It seems as if the whole of humanity has lost its way.

In the absence of leadership, education, civility, and common decency—the "wonders" of technology have come along and hijacked our attention, rendering us little more than spectators trained to consume.

Speeding through existence—barely skimming the surface—we wonder why our lives seem superficial, unsatisfying, and unreal. Many of us feel detached from the planet, ourselves, and each other.

We don't realize this state of affairs persists because we *agree* that it does.

Whether we agree to *this* or we agree to *that* doesn't matter—we are agreeing to an *outside* reality—a media reality, a popular reality, someone *else's* reality, simply because we haven't been taught or encouraged to wake up and think for ourselves.

The answers to our problems are simple, but each individual must rise to the occasion for themselves.

If you feel like you're asleep, underwater, discouraged, defeated, lost, lonely, disheartened, hopeless, drugged, victimized, and/or addicted to things you know are unhealthy—I understand.

I have felt every one of these things at times. I believe we all have.

I was never beaten as a child. Never went hungry. I never worried about money—or whether I'd have a comfortable bed to sleep in. But I was disregarded. No one around me offered genuine interest in who I was or what I was going through, which led me to feel increasingly lost, alone, and terribly, terribly sad.

I think many people feel this way: ignored. In our current, highly narcissistic society, many of us suffer from not being seen or heard by a real-live, caring human being.

From a very young age, I turned to nature for comfort. And through that cherished relationship with the natural world, I discovered a connection to my own inner spirit. I learned to heal myself. I learned how to be whole. And so can you.

What is turmoil but a demand for change? What is an existential crisis but the opportunity to get back in touch with our values, meaning, and purpose—a signal to adopt actions and a direction that will lead us to a life we can be proud of?

We are being called upon to stop looking *outside* ourselves for answers, validation, and even love. We have reached a time in history when it is imperative for us to discover our own autonomy as beings. To heal ourselves, parent ourselves, love ourselves, and, most importantly, *listen* to ourselves. By "ourselves," I don't mean the incessant chatter of our self-centered egos, but rather the trust-worthy counsel of our soul—which is there, waiting for us to be still, breathe into our hearts, and listen.

By listening to our own inner guidance, we have the opportunity to create our lives in concert with our higher selves and, in so doing, with the best in each other. This is what's meant by oneness, by wholeness—by unity. This is what's meant by awakening consciousness.

The chaos we're experiencing both individually and collectively is a sign of the times. It is summoning a new way to move forward. The time is: *now*. The question is: *how?*

Time to Wake Up

The answer is so simple it's difficult to believe: wake up!

Turn off all the noise. Ignore all the "influences," and connect to your own inner truth. The Law of Attraction is real. We *are* what we *believe*. We need to wake up and take responsibility for our thinking and what the hell we're placing our attention on. We need to understand and believe that a universal truth lies within each and every one of us. And we need to *believe* that truth into existence.

When we seek counsel from what we know in our own heart—and *act* on that truth—we move toward a higher state of humanity. This is the nature of evolution. This is why we're here! Our peril contains a message: *it's time to wake up and realize who you are and what you're capable of.*

Artists have always been our greatest opinion leaders. Artists are possessed by a need to reflect on what we're capable of beyond the day-to-day grind that dulls our senses and lures us into a collective sleep. This book is a humble attempt to wake up the artist in everyone—to connect you to your own source of inspiration and the solutions that live in the ether, waiting for you to tune in and listen.

If this book calls out to you, it is not because it offers answers to your most intimate questions, but because it offers stories and lessons that might lead you to discover those answers for yourself.

My goal is to help people uncover the very best in themselves—who you really are and what you are capable of when you listen to your own inherent knowledge. The book offers some age-old, very simple disciplines you can practice daily that will set you on the road to recovering your own autonomy.

My dream is to inspire people to contribute to the whole of human-kind, each in their own unique way. I believe the most important thing in life is acting on what we know in our own heart to be true. If I can help others do that a bit more, I will have served a purpose.

My Story Begins and Ends with Acting

I am an actor's daughter. My father, Henry Jones, was a character actor whose Broadway career peaked in 1958 with a Tony Award for his performance in *Sunrise at Campobello.* In the play, Henry played Louis Howe, friend and advisor to Franklin Delano Roosevelt.

I was eight years old when it opened. I remember sitting fourth-row center, staring up at the grown-ups play-acting like children. To my young eyes, it looked like they were cavorting in a giant doll-house. It still looks that way to me. A well-done play has a magic about it. I feel blessed to have grown up surrounded by the spirited people of that world. I loved their flamboyance, their humor, and their grown-up love of make-believe.

After my parents divorced, my father moved to Hollywood, where his life revolved around television and film work. Although "Henry Jones" wasn't exactly a well-known name, he supported our family through acting jobs alone. When he worked, we splurged on theatre tickets and dinners out. When jobs were scarce, supper might consist of a tuna sandwich or chicken noodle soup.

Everything about Hollywood seemed larger than life. To my young eyes, it was like living in a movie. The houses were mansions, the women glamorous, the men charming—even the freeways were triple the size of anything I'd ever seen—big roads leading to big dreams.

It seemed to me that all the superstars I met had two things in common:

1. Each and every one of them displayed a level of confidence I'd never seen before.

2. They seemed to have made themselves up out of thin air, manifesting an image and personality that resided somewhere in their imaginations. They became the person they dreamed of becoming. They did in their lives what they did in their work: they created a life of their own imagining—beautiful and dramatic.

I learned this truth: *acting is about creating a life where there once was none. It's about manifesting!*

I have been an acting teacher most of my adult life. I've taught actors who've starred in movies and television, people who've never set foot on a stage before, and every level in between. I've served as a creative consultant to some of the biggest movie stars in the world, and I've taught people with no innate talent for the job, helping them find confidence in their process and fulfillment in their careers.

In my thirty years of teaching, my intention has always been to offer techniques that will help actors connect to and flush out their best ideas. I engage them in ongoing conversations about the following:

- The benefits of a positive attitude

- Comporting themselves as a professional

- Imaginative administration

- Commitment to finishing the job

- The benefits of daily ritual

- The nature of inspiration

- And the inspiration of nature

I also talk to actors about the importance of intention in their work and that class begins and ends with *intending* to become the best person you can be.

I train actors to *know* that they know. I believe confidence is as simple as that: *knowing* that you know how to go about a thing.

Because actors sometimes get caught up in self-absorbed thinking, I offer practices to bend their interest toward concerns *outside* themselves. My intention is to give them tools that help ease them out of their carefully crafted personas in order to view the world from their *heart* as opposed to their head. I like to remind them: *a star shines not to bask in the glory of its own heat but to illuminate others.*

Actors

The actor as an artist is a seeker of souls

He wants to be *the hand*

He wants to be all *the hands*

He has a hunger to understand the nature of life

And is never as alive *as when in the throes of* being *someone else*

The actor is out to discover how life begins

By creating it himself again and again and again

Actors wear their insides out, reflecting for us the depth and breadth of the human condition. It's as if one life isn't enough for them. They want to conjure multiple lives before our very eyes.

When we see a performance we love, it lifts our spirit. We literally begin vibrating at a higher frequency, which invites us to leave our seats and *enter* the story. The actor is so real he transports us to another existence, and we take a little vacation from our own.

And when we return, feeling refreshed from our time away, don't we sometimes feel like, "Wow! If they can create that much life out of thin air—commanding thoughts, feelings, and behaviors at will—surely I can do a little better with my own?"

In this way, actors touch a kindred spirit in us all. Something in their work feels familiar, inspiring us to reach for more. Because actors create life in the moment, they have something to teach us all.

The more I explored the acting techniques I offer, the more I saw that they could apply to anyone interested in discovering and maintaining access to inspiration and the power of calling upon that connection at will.

Growing Up with Art and Artists

My father was an actor, my mother a photographer, and my step-father a writer. I grew up in one of the many artists' colonies scattered along the Hudson River Valley, often referred to as the Landing.

Clustered along a narrow, wooded road winding its way down to the river sits a collection of houses—some old, a couple new, a few dating back to the eighteenth century. On snowy winter nights, when the trees stand bare, the lights in the windows make the houses stand out like ornaments on a Christmas tree.

By mid-July, these houses hide behind the thick flora of ancient trees, an overgrowth of honeysuckle, and poison ivy—a metaphor for my experiences growing up there.

Because of the hamlet's proximity to Manhattan, an abundance of world-class artists have always inhabited the place. Country living grounds these luminaries, adding a sane contrast to the challenges of their celebrity existence in the limelight.

I remember these legends of the Landing gathered around our dining table, talking about their process and relationship with art. The painters were in a class of their own. They were different from the performing artists. They seemed anti-glamour, anti-fashion, and anti-establishment. Unlike performing artists, they weren't tasked with creating art before your eyes. Instead, at least in the '60s and '70s, they seemed transfixed on elevating the ordinary—something I became deeply interested in and that cropped up in my teaching later in life.

Point being, whether on the East Coast or the West, I spent my formative years studying a broad array of artists. Artists of all kinds. Artists at the top of their game. When they were into their work, they seemed lit from within—filled with joy and purpose. When they talked about a project, they led with enthusiasm. As long as they were involved in the creative process, they seemed happier and more authentic than in their everyday selves.

And when the project was over, they seemed to suffer a loss. They'd fall into doubt, wondering whether they could conjure all that magic again. It was as if they were going through withdrawal from the high of all that creativity.

I wanted to know more about that phenomenon. I wanted to know:

- Why do people become artists?

- What makes them different?

- What is their process?

- What are their problems?

- What makes them happy—*when* they are happy?

- And why did some of them take themselves out of the game completely?

Over years of observing, I developed a strong suspicion that an artist's *best* work didn't come from their head. In fact, it wasn't intellectual at all. An artist's best work seemed to come from their heart vibrating in unison with some higher, larger force. And with this unity came a passion. A sense of purpose. An enthusiasm for life. A devotion.

Boy, was I interested in that!

Just exactly what was that light I saw within greatness? It seemed to me of a spiritual nature. I would spend my life's work dedicated to understanding it.

Where Does It All Come From?

When their work is going well, artists feel *plugged into something*. Something that produces an energy not there before. Call it vision, call it the muse, call it inspiration—I call it spirit.

Spirit, God, muse, angels, guides, entities—these words and concepts can turn people off. Some people will bristle just reading this. It's as if these concepts have been hijacked by religious authorities and are not trustworthy anymore.

Awakening the spirit within is different. It is a deeply personal, one-on-one matter. This vital lifeline between you and *you* should be kept private and protected from other people's opinion, interpretation, invalidation, or alteration.

When I'm teaching, I refer to this energy exchange as *impulse* or *intuition* because I realize the concept of spirit-inspired art can be a little much for some.

But I challenge any artist to look at the four o'clock light streaming through a grove of redwoods, listen to the sound of water cascading over rocks, get drunk on the cherry blossoms in Central Park, eat a perfect peach, or dance under the northern lights on an island in Maine—I challenge them to *inhale* the miracles of nature and not feel a kindred spirit well up in them. When we take the time to observe and be touched by the power of nature, something moves in us. Something exciting. Something that feels familiar, like the best of us, like home.

There is a sleeping giant available to *anyone* who wishes to co-create either an acting role or the life of their dreams—no difference.

Getting to know that place within is one of the most *personal* things we do. Acknowledge and admire this spirit within, and your relationship will expand exponentially.

Exercise:
Expanding into Unimaginable Truth

Throughout this book, I will offer meditations, exercises, and journaling prompts that will help you enter the present moment and open up a conversation with your heart.

Here's a fun way to feel connected to something greater than yourself. Stretch out on your bed, close your eyes, and consider this:

You are lying on a bed

In a room

In a city

On a planet

Which is spinning around at 1,000 miles per hour

While flying around the sun at 66,000 miles per hour

As our solar system circles the Milky Way at 450,000 miles per hour

*And you are but one of more than seven billion human souls
speeding through the cosmos*

*While seven other planets—also spinning, also revolving
around the sun*

*Create exactly the right amount of gravity to keep the Earth
in a stable orbit*

And you snug in your bed

There we are! All of us whirling through the galaxy at an unimaginable speed. In perfect balance. Once you wake up to that, you've made a great start in appreciating the vastness of the spirit within. You've found wonder in what just a moment ago seemed ordinary and mundane.

Just as a benevolent force keeps the planets spinning in perfect order, the very same force keeps us on track as well.

To connect to the spirit within is to feel whole—in one deep breath, to realize we are complete. To connect to this power is to realize you *have*, have *always* had, and will *always* have indisputable inner guidance.

The moment you realize you can tune into that force is the moment you understand: YOU *are* that force, and you're *designed* to create the life of your dreams by listening to your heart. Coming to this understanding is like opening a long-lost letter from your higher self. Coming into this power is our destiny.

To connect to the spirit within is to never feel lonely again.

Your Connection to Spirit

Artists *live* to create. An artist in the act of creating is in ecstasy. They will tell you *creating* is their greatest joy.

I got to thinking one day—if the connection to inspiration/muse/spirit always brings joy, then we *should* be able to reverse engineer it. In other words, if the moment of inspiration is always connected to joy, can we *consciously* create joy as a means to live a more inspired and artful life?

I believe the answer is yes. Using the same techniques and exercises I give actors, I believe *anyone* can discover and connect to their own depth of joy. And because joy vibrates at such a high frequency, it opens us up to a more creative and inspired life.

This book is dedicated to helping you connect to and expand that source of inspiration—not just because the capacity to do so will elevate both life and art, but because in doing so, I am introducing you to your most powerful ally: YOU!

Not the you who you *think* you are. Not the personality you've spent your lifetime cultivating and are now so understandably attached to. Not the you who is wrapped up in the continuous worry, drama, and negative thinking we often addict ourselves to. Instead, I'm talking about the YOU who is waiting inside this marvelous equipment (body, mind, and spirit) to create the life *you* came here to live.

I want to help you locate and befriend the YOU who is an artist capable of manifesting anything.

By sharing my stories, I want to illustrate how the most challenging events of our lives are there to guide us to a higher perspective, to our next lesson, to our next evolution, to an awakening of our best self—particularly when we embrace them as such.

People used to look up to artists not because of their popularity or personality but because of their special relationship with the muse. Actors, musicians, writers, painters, and dancers can wake up that harmonic in us, and we *feel* a connection moving quietly within. We feel inspired because they are inspired.

An inspired artist awakens our enthusiasm and interest in new things. Things *outside* ourselves. Those feelings may not last long, particularly if we don't know how to cultivate them, but we know we felt *something*, we felt *better*—we felt *right* somehow. If only we could feel that way all the time.

I believe we can. At least, I believe we can do a whole lot better.

- I believe art is the expression of a person who thinks for themselves.

- I believe there is art in everyone.

- I believe we are spirit in body, having an ingenious game with all this marvelous sensory equipment, and our nature is to grow, expand, and ascend to higher versions of ourselves.

- I believe in the art of living and that the simple act of making an egg for breakfast can be elevated to an artful gesture.

- I believe we are meant to create our lives with guidance from our higher selves, and we locate that connection by becoming still and turning our attention inward.

- I believe there's no better way to shift our world toward a more benevolent and unified collection of souls than for each of us to *exercise* and expand this intimate relationship to the spirit within, thereby living in coherence with our own heart.

This book is about luring, cultivating, and nurturing that profoundly personal connection as you draw upon the artist in you to create and manifest a life of your own making. If all of us strengthen our personal connection to this sacred place within, I believe we can manifest a soulful evolution of humankind rather than a sad extinction.

If you are an actor, if you are an artist, if you are someone seeking the tools to help you to create a more fulfilling, joyous, and artful life, well then, this book—which bears the seeds of my own lessons—this book is for *you*.

CHAPTER 1

The Journey Begins with a Goal

"Quiet the mind, and the soul will speak."

—MA JAYA SATI BHAGAVATI

MY EARLIEST YEARS WERE SPENT IN NEW HOPE, PENNSYLVANIA, A small-town artists' community where life was very different for children than it is today. We had much less fear and tremendous freedom. We had next to no TV and much more playing. We had fewer things and none of the electronic "conveniences" that suck up our attention today. Consequently, we lived in real-time, as opposed to creating a virtual life.

Hard as it is to believe, at the age of five years old, my best friend, Peter Daily, and I had the run of the town. Our playground was a little over a square mile, with the Delaware River on one side— filled with snakes (for real), and stones, and puppy dog bones (meaning we would spend hours throwing stuff into the river for Peter's dogs to retrieve)—and the ominous Delaware Canal on the other. The freedom was exhilarating for a five-year-old.

We weren't supposed to play on the towpath that ran alongside the canal, but there was way too much adventure up there for us to pay attention to any rules. Canals, barges, railroad tracks, trains, rivers, bridges, gardens, grasses, trees, breezes, blizzards, abandoned houses, skating on rivers, floods, raccoons, and running through forests played such a significant part in my early childhood that they still show up in my dreams as symbols to be unlocked.

At five years old, Peter and I were actively discovering ourselves through an independent relationship with nature and our immediate surroundings.

The one thing we were forbidden to do was to cross the Lambertville Bridge—which at 1,000 feet was a nice stroll on a Sunday afternoon for tourists—but to a five-year-old, it was the longest bridge known to man. It was the bridge to the BIG city.

Lambertville was actually a small city in Hunterdon County, New Jersey. But in our young imaginations, it was big and bad, and anything could happen there—as opposed to New Hope, directly across the river, which was a tiny, touristy borough in Bucks County, Pennsylvania.

Of course, we did cross that bridge one day. Peter and I had made a pact that we'd brave the adventure the minute we felt old enough. As it turned out, circumstances caused us to push the goal forward, making the expedition that much more exciting.

Rumor had it there was a first-rate candy store on the other side of the bridge, and Peter and I had been saving up for a splurge. The day Peter broke the news that his family was moving to Ohio, we decided it was time. We cracked open our piggy banks, threw the coins in a sack, and walked from my house to the bridge without speaking.

Looking across to the other side was terrifying. The bridge seemed to sway in the wind, and the cars coming into New Hope were bumper to bumper—Saturday tourists. The pedestrian walkway was crowded as well. I imagined the bridge would collapse under the weight of all those cars and people, or worse, I'd be blown off and carried away in the wind.

Peter and I looked at each other, exposing our terror. And then, in the same moment, we took a deep breath, turned toward the bridge, and ran as fast as we could—dodging and weaving through the Saturday lookie-loos to get to the other side.

Sure enough, there was the candy store, right there on the first block, with a dazzling array of goodness. We got as much candy as our money would buy, which seemed like enough for a couple of years, then scampered back across the bridge to safety.

We had Fireballs and Turkish Taffy, Charleston Chews and Root Beer Barrels, Cherry Slices and Clark Bars, Good & Plenty and bubble gum cigarettes—which we thought were the coolest!— and we had one Donald Duck PEZ dispenser, which we fought over until Peter gave it to me as a parting gift. It was Halloween in July.

Now, all we had to do was figure out where to celebrate. Since he was moving, Peter let me in on a secret: his father had a room in the basement where he'd go to smoke cigarettes. His dad was at work, and Peter knew how to break in. We grabbed some Cokes from his kitchen fridge (something you would never in a million years find at my house) and headed for the basement with our loot. There, in that disgusting, dank, basement cave, we gorged on candy and Cokes until we felt sick, all the while flipping through *Playboy* magazines—which I found disgusting and fascinating in equal measure. I rolled home with a stomachache, leaving the rest of the candy with Peter. I was done with the contraband. The big adventure seemed surprisingly unfulfilling in the end.

That was the last time I saw Peter Daily. His family moved shortly thereafter. But even at five years old, we had achieved what appeared to be the biggest, bravest goal we could muster: to cross the longest bridge in the world and retrieve the treasure from the other side!

In the end, it wasn't the goal that was important—it was the journey. It was facing our fear, exploring our boundaries, and surpassing our limits. It was flying across that bridge as fast as my five-year-old legs could carry me. The goal is what sets the journey in motion.

Setting Goals

Fulfilling a series of mindful goals, one after another, is what puts us in the driver's seat of our own lives.

I think contribution is the most valuable aspiration of all. The question then becomes, "Does this goal/choice/ambition/wish *contribute* in some way? Does it contribute to my art? My life? My health? My loved ones? My community?"

When we make our choices in this way, we discover what's important to us. We gain confidence in our direction. We feel more awake. We rise to the challenges of our own intentions. We learn to set worthier goals, which lead to more constructive choices and more expansive journeys.

Your job is then to stay the course, cultivate a positive attitude, keep taking action, and, most importantly, *move forward exactly as if you have already achieved the goal!*

When you operate as if you've already achieved your goal and *do* the things you'd do if you'd already succeeded—the Universe will respond in kind. The Law of Attraction is real. It works by frequency. Simply put, you draw to you the mirror image of the energy you radiate out. Similar frequencies attract like magnets. Smile, and you'll soon have something to smile about. Worry about your job, and the Universe will bring you circumstances that will help you worry even more.

Many of us live in a perpetual state of "I want." When we continuously *want* something, instead of attracting the object of our desire, the Universe will bring us everything we need to help us *want* it more. This works in ways both little and large. In other words, don't pray for peace—it reflects the lack of it. Instead, *be* the peace you wish for in the world. It's a simple but profound shift in your point of view:

- I don't *want* to be an actor. I *am* an actor because every day, I do the things actors do.

- I don't *want* to be a writer. I *am* a writer because I write every day.

- I don't *want* to be an organ grinder. I *am* an organ grinder because I grind the organ every chance I get. Plus, I bought a monkey and named him Marcel.

Once you know what your goal is and you are doing the activities of that aspiration daily, give yourself permission to *be* your goal. The Universe will respond in kind. Every journey begins with a single step. Commit to walking the road every day, and the journey has begun. Believe in walking the road every day, and you *become* the road.

We are each on our own journey, whether or not we consciously contribute to the direction of its flow. Wherever we are in life, we have arrived there by our thoughts and actions. As such, we are in *exactly* the right place to learn our next lesson. Sometimes, we make the leap, learn the lesson, and change. Sometimes, there's more to learn, more to accept, and more to understand before we can move forward. Either way, there is *always* a lesson. There is always the opportunity to learn, grow, awaken, and expand—that's why we're here.

My big adventure with Peter taught me that scoring the best candy in the world might not have been the worthiest goal—but stepping out of my comfort zone and crossing the longest bridge in the world was. It taught me that bridges are there to be crossed—and that I was braver and stronger than I'd ever imagined!

The Actor's Goal

The actor's goal is always the same: "*I want to get the job.*" It often keeps them from doing their best work because their intention is off. Their intention (goal) is to *get the job*. My counsel is always the following: "Shift your intention. The goal is not to get the job. The goal is to do your best work by making it personal." Actors need to shift their thinking from "I want the part" to "I *am* the part."

I tell them, "Your best work is measured by how personal you make it and how much you commit to your choices. One hundred percent is always recognized as undeniable. Whether you get the part or not, the goal is always the same: give 100 percent of *you*! Then, if you get the job, great! If not, you'll be remembered as a first-rate actor, and they'll call you in again."

My counsel is always to ask the right questions. Make choices that move you. Enter the work through the character's goals. Be a person, not an actor.

That's pretty good advice for anyone: *Ask the right questions. Make choices that move you. Give 100 percent of your best self. Be an authentic person rather than an idea of yourself.*

Make the Goal Personal

Because the actor's goal is always to *get the job*, they deliver what they *think* is wanted. What's odd is that most of the actors who audition for a part will play some version of the same thing. They take their cues from the words on the page and say them with as much emotion as they can muster. I call it "words squared." There is no dimension to the acting because the actor hasn't given himself to the part.

> *You can't be an artist and worry about what others think!*
>
> *You can't be your own person and worry about what others think, either*
>
> *Embrace the freedom that comes with trusting yourself*
>
> *Discover and claim your own point of view about* everything
>
> *Become your own person, and you'll stop caring about what others think*
>
> *Become your own person by trusting and following your own good intentions*

Even well-trained actors have trouble remembering that their best work is always the goal.

Actors have trouble letting go of "I gotta figure out what they want in order to book this job!"

The funny thing is, most of the time, *they* (the people in charge of hiring you) don't know what they want. They are waiting for the actor to bring them something special, something personal, something not already on the page. They want to be enchanted. *They* are thinking, "I'll know what I want when I see it."

What *they* want is simple:

- They want to be inspired by something bigger than themselves.

- They want the magic of an actor living in an imaginary moment as if it were real.

- They want to be transported out of their humdrum reality.

- They want the artist to do what they don't have the courage to do—expose themselves.

- They want the artist to contribute to the project and make it better in some way.

Can you see how this applies to you? How much of *yourself* do you offer? Are you seeking your own point of view? Honestly, what are your intentions? Are you striving to be liked, admired, safe, or hired? Or is your intention to give the best of what *you*—uniquely—have to contribute?

Meditation and Journaling

The purpose of this book is to offer you techniques that will lead you to the peace and confidence you'll experience when connected to your most essential self. I recommend making it a goal to practice daily, if only for ten minutes.

Let's take a closer look at why you may want to adopt these two practices for yourself.

Why Meditation?

I had a medical crisis a while back; my blood pressure was high, and my doctor wanted to put me on medication to bring it down. I avoid pharmaceuticals like the plague, so I told him I wanted six months to lower my numbers via lifestyle choices. After a lecture on the risks of stroke, he acquiesced.

I did some research. I discovered that high blood sugar and high blood pressure are connected. My condition made sense, as I'd been indulging in sweets and carbohydrates, eating for comfort rather than health. So, the first thing I did was change my diet. I started to *eat* the plants I admired so much.

I also read stories about people who had lowered their blood pressure with meditation. I have to admit, I didn't want to meditate. I thought I'd be terrible at it. I had a very fast and very active mind. I couldn't imagine gaining control over it, much less slowing it down. Furthermore, I was attached to my thinking. I identified with it. It felt familiar and fit my personality. In all honesty, I *love* thinking!

But I did it anyway. I took a beginning mindfulness meditation class and practiced for twenty minutes every day. Within four months, between diet and meditation, my blood pressure dropped to normal. More importantly, meditation brought me to the present moment, quieted my obsessive thinking, and led me to a more authentic life. It gave me a much-needed break from "myself" and, in so doing, created more space. With the expansion came more possibility.

Meditation Apps

Download a free meditation app on your phone. (I recommend Insight Timer, but there are many.)

- Spend a few minutes getting to know your new app.

- Set the timer at ten minutes for when you want to simply sit in meditation.

- Seek out and use the heart symbol to "bookmark" at least one of each of the following:

  * A guided meditation

  * A chanting meditation, like "Om" or "Sa Ta Na Ma"

  * Sounds of nature, such as water over rocks, wind, ocean waves, or crickets

  * A 528Hz healing frequency to "sit" with

You may also find you prefer to sit in "silence," allowing the life around you to make itself known through sound.

I encourage you to try all kinds of meditation.

There are also a myriad of wonderful classes, books, online resources, and phone apps you can explore. Many of these are free.

Find out what moves you. Happy hunting!

To a certain degree, I believed I *was* my thinking. My thinking was proof of my existence. But...

> *By sitting quietly and connecting to my breath*
>
> *By observing my thoughts and noting their* quality
>
> *Whether it be planning (a favorite of mine)*
>
> *Or judgment*
>
> *Or worry*
>
> *Or some other category of habitual thinking*
>
> *I'd simply* note *the thought*
>
> *And go back to my breath*

In this way, I discovered that I am the *observer*. I am a *presence* observing my breath.

When you observe your breath without thinking, you ease into the presence that is YOU. You are that invisible energy that is awareness. Since the observer/presence has no physical form, many people call this consciousness *spirit*. To locate this most essential self, you need only to still yourself by connecting to breath.

When you breathe into your heart, you activate the innate intelligence that is *you*.

What a peaceful feeling such connection affords. It feels like nothing and everything, all at the same time—like perfect balance. It feels like truth so distilled that even a tiny sliver of it—say, meditating ten minutes a day on a regular basis—is a game-changer.

Most of us don't know how to *be*. I know I didn't. I had to be taught. We are *beings* who are learning how to *be*. Think of meditation as mental hygiene, a time to relax into *being*.

If you want more control of your life—if you want more joy, focus, peace, connection, and authenticity—there is no easier way to find it than through the practice of daily meditation.

Regular practice will bring you many things, including:

- Increased focus

- Deeper relaxation

- Control over anxiety

- Help with pain management

- Lower blood pressure

- Alleviation of depression

- Improved sleep

- Enhanced self-awareness

- Promotion of kindness and compassion

Not only did meditation normalize my blood pressure, it also changed my life. Truth became something I could measure with my own inner barometer. Most importantly, the breath of my higher consciousness found a channel into my life.

The Value of Journaling

There are as many forms of journaling as there are people, and as with all ritual, consistency and duration make the benefits known. Everyone who's ever kept a journal will tell you: giving yourself the time and space to have an honest conversation between you and YOU is an illuminating practice.

The meditations and exercises you encounter within these pages will include a number of journaling prompts. Use them as you see fit. If journaling is already part of your daily life, feel free to adapt these offerings to your liking.

I suggest that actors journal:

- About their observations

- As their character

- To manifest their goals

- To solve problems

- To understand emotions

All of these topics will engage the artist in anyone and lead you to discovery.

Find your own way with the prompts offered. Remember, there is no right or wrong in journaling. There's no right or wrong in art or meditation, either.

Beginning the Practice

Find a notebook with clean pages and a good feel. Find a nice pen, one that moves well. You might like to put together a shoebox of art supplies. Include a small scissor and some glue to cut and paste images of things you'd like to manifest. Maybe you like to work with colored pens or crayons.

Look for a picture of yourself as a child that you *love*—then tuck it into your journal.

Now, find a special place in your home. A quiet space where you can be alone. A sacred space, if you will. You may want to include a special pillow to sit on. A candle. Maybe a crystal, flower, stone, or shell. Experiment with essential oils. Collect inspired reading materials. Make it simple, and make it your own.

Start your practice by committing to meditate ten minutes a day for the next month.

Whether you are sitting on the floor, in a chair, or cross-legged on your bed—sit upright, relaxing your shoulders back and down. Send your tail bone toward earth—and the crown of your head toward the sky. Create space by gently moving them apart. You will feel this in your solar plexus.

The Meditation

Close your eyes, and breathe into your heart.

>**Inhale:** I breathe in stillness.

>**Exhale:** I breathe out peace—I smile.

Repeat for ten minutes.

When thoughts come up, note "thinking" and go back to your breath. There is no wrong way to meditate. It's a practice. Every time you turn your attention from thinking back to your breath, you are being mindful. Like flexing a muscle, you are strengthening mindfulness.

>*There is a space*

>*Available to us in stillness*

>*A place balanced on the tip of zero*

>*A sacred gap between thoughts*

>*Where the mind stands still*

>*And if we wish*

>*We can retrieve what we already know*

After practicing a while, you'll be able to still yourself and come to the present moment in a breath or two. Nothing could be more valuable.

We are meant for these times; that's why we're here. We are waking up!

Exercise:
Journaling with Your Inner Child

After ten minutes of meditation, do the following:

- Lift the picture of yourself as a child out of the journal and take it in.

- Breathe into your heart.

- Exhale—breathe your love into the heart of the child in the picture.

- Spend a few more breaths here.

- Ask the child to tell you three things they'd like you to know.

- Listen without judgment.

- Then, write down what you hear. If you don't hear anything, just put your pen to paper and begin writing. Don't stop. Write straight through until there's nothing more to say.

Almost everyone has an inner child who longs for something they never received or has something to say that was silenced. Since our inner child is in charge of our spirit of play, it's a good idea to keep them happy. Unburden them when necessary; otherwise, they get cranky—or worse, morose. You may want to give your inner child an ongoing voice in your journal by writing letters to each other when the spirit moves you.

Healing the wounds of our inner child is our job now. This writing prompt is a way to re-parent and integrate a hurt child by listening with unconditional love. Their feelings need to be respected, not judged or "fixed." Love them, listen to them, acknowledge their feelings, care for their needs—but keep this in mind: wounded children make bad decisions. They want to smoke, drink, act out, and carry on in unhealthy ways. They often choose friends and lovers who reflect their grievances. Understand them, love them up, but never give them the keys to the car. Never put a pissed-off kid in charge of anything in your life.

Make it a goal to journal daily. Even ten minutes a day of jotting down what you're grateful for is a tremendous gift to give yourself.

Make it a goal to meditate daily. Even ten minutes a day is a gift you give to your soul.

Both of these practices will enhance your confidence in the pursuit of your goals. Try it for a month and tell me what you think. Your journey begins with a goal.

CHAPTER 2

Thinking You Know vs. Knowing You Know

"It takes courage to grow up and become who you really are."

—E.E. CUMMINGS

WHEN I WAS GROWING UP IN NEW HOPE, WE LIVED NEXT DOOR TO A man named Tom Cannell. His house was falling down, and his lawn, which ran parallel to ours, was a jungle of wild grasses. He had lost his legs during the war, and in fair weather, he would roll out of his house in a rickety wooden wheelchair, with what looked like a threadbare tartan draped over his lap. Often, he'd sit out on his porch for the better part of the day, staring out at nothing.

My six-year-old "bones" told me he was a sweet, sad, and lonely man—but my brother, David, who is four years older than I am, told me Tom Cannell kept a gun in his lap.

"It's right under that gross red rug that covers his stubs," he said. "If you ever cross the property line and step on Tom Cannell's lawn, he will pull out his gun and shoot you dead on the spot!"

I looked at my brother like, *I know you are making this up*—but he doubled down on *be afraid, be very, **very** afraid.*

My brother was ten years old, practically a grown-up as far as I could tell, so instead of my heart going out to poor Tom Cannell, as my instincts told me to, I started viewing him in a whole new light—he was a monster with a gun, and I became terrified of the man.

The problem was that David and I often played on our lawn, which ran parallel to his. I always checked to see if old Tom Cannell was out on his porch—and if he was, I'd try to steer clear of the place—but my brother liked to torture me. He took to "accidentally" tossing my toys over the property line, and there was no way for me to retrieve them without getting shot by Tom Cannell.

It all began with my brand-new baton, which my brother stole and began twirling to taunt me. He then escalated the tease by tossing it up to catch it. Of course, it landed in the tall, snake-infested grasses of Tom Cannell's lawn. I was furious! How was I to become a majorette and march in the Fourth of July Parade with all the other girls if I couldn't practice my baton? David, on the other hand, was delighted to see how terrified I was and took every opportunity to "accidentally" lose more stuff: half of a tuna sandwich I was enjoying, my hula hoop…even one of my favorite red sneakers "somehow" ended up across that invisible, but very real, property line.

I lay in bed at night, planning a sneak attack to capture the hostages—all those toys lost to the weeds! But in the end, I just scared myself and ended up with nightmares.

After my favorite doll ended up in the jungle, I went to my father in tears. "Daddy, David threw my Betsy doll on Tom Cannell's lawn and—"

My father cut me off. "Mr. Cannell," he corrected.

"Yeah, well, David threw Betsy over there, and she probably broke into a million pieces!" I sobbed.

I love my dad, but he was not especially sympathetic to the concerns of small children. I don't think he even looked up from the paper as he said, "Cry quietly, dear."

Cry quietly? Are you kidding?! I wondered if anyone would cry after I was lying dead in the grass from a gunshot wound to the heart, my doll in my arms, the snakes crawling over us both.

David was born on February 26, and I was born on February 24, four years later. Forever after, our birthdays would be celebrated on February 25. Neither one of us felt great about the arrangement.

On my sixth birthday, I got a baby carriage, which I thought was just about the best present ever! And David got a bow and arrow set. Do you see where this is going?

I was out on the lawn playing with my new baby carriage. Tom Cannell was nowhere in sight, thank God. And my brother was up in the giant tree outside my bedroom window, eyes on my new pram, which had a bonnet, making it look—I have to admit—a little bit like a covered wagon.

Suddenly, I looked up to see David with an arrow trained on the bonnet of my new pram!

I screamed! He screamed! He leaped out of the tree, firing arrows at my baby carriage as fast as he possibly could. I had to abandon the thing and all my babies as we were right at the very edge of Tom Cannell's lawn, and, well, it was all too dangerous.

Frustrated that his arrows were not *penetrating* the hood of the baby carriage, David picked them up and started stabbing my precious new toy. I screamed my head off at the unfairness of it all—right when Tom Cannell rolled out, wondering what all the fuss was about.

He was just in time to see the baby carriage tip over, spilling my entire doll collection over his snake-infested lawn. David looked back at me in shock, realizing he'd stepped over the line in more ways than one. I looked at him, bawling my eyes out. Then we both took off, fast as we could, away from Tom Cannell's gun and into my father's office to plead our case.

"But Daddy, David stabbed…" overlapped with "The carriage fell on my arrows."

But all my father heard was, "And Tom Cannell's gonna shoot me dead with the gun he has under his blanket."

My father took me gently by the hand and walked my brother and me over to Mr. Cannell's house to properly introduce us.

Tom Cannell was a shy man. He was kind enough to offer us cookies—which I did *not* want—but as he wheeled around to go inside and get them, the old threadbare blanket slipped, and I could see he didn't have a gun under there after all. Just stubs.

We sat on the porch—my brother, my father, and me—eating stale cookies with the sad, shy man who had no legs and no one to love him. I was no longer afraid and, instead, felt a depth of compassion I couldn't fathom at that age—like tears running down my insides.

My instincts had been right all along! Tom Cannell was a sad, sweet, and lonely man, one who came to life that day by rising to the occasion of our visit.

It was my first lesson in believing what you know in your heart to be true. I had given up what I *felt* about old Tom Cannell and believed what my brother *thought* instead, simply because he was four years older. I believed him because it was easier than standing up for myself, and something about that conflict struck me even at that young age.

Every day thereafter, when I saw Tom Cannell on the porch, I'd wave. "Hey, Mr. Cannell!" I'd yell on my way to school. And he'd wave back with a smile. I vowed never again to underestimate another person by believing what somebody else thought about them.

I had been right: I *knew* in my heart Tom Cannell was a good man. At best, my brother *thought* he knew better, but my guess is the only thing he *knew* was he wanted to mess with me, as older brothers sometimes do.

Thinking vs. Knowing

Thinking and knowing are two different things. *Thinking that you know* is an intellectual pursuit. It involves the personality packing away information as proof of being righter, brighter, and better.

Thinking is a miraculous tool. We manifest our lives with thought. We generate emotions with thought. We reflect on our experiences with thought. We even create time with thought: *I was there, now I'm here, and I'd like to end up somewhere else.* Past, present, and future.

Thinking is a terrific part of the equipment! But for most of us, our thinking is *way* out of balance. We don't remember how to stop. We think so much that we think we *are* our thoughts—we don't *know* who we are without them.

Knowing that you know, on the other hand, is a visceral feeling. It has nothing to do with thought. *Knowing* lives in certainty, and certainty lives in the heart (often we feel it in our gut), but when we *know*, we *feel* it—and the more we acknowledge the connection, the more certain we become.

Thinking You Know

We seem to be—artists and everyone else in the world—in the business of *knowing*. At least we *think* we are. There's a desperation to "know." The more we know, the better we are. The more we know, the safer we are. The more we know, the smarter we are. Forget *trusting*; we need to *know*!

In fact, we *think* we need to "know" because the more we know, the *righter* we are. The need to be right rules us. But grasping at what we *think* we know, in order to prove ourselves right, isn't knowing at all.

Oddly, artists are actually in the business of *not* knowing. Only when we suspend our need to know are we capable of *discovering*. Without discovery, there is nothing new to express. Without discovery, there is no thinking for yourself. Without discovery, there's no *art*.

Andy Warhol, icon of the Pop Art movement, discovered a new way to look at our culture through his silkscreens of Campbell's Soup cans as well as his diptych of Marilyn Monroe. He is likely the first artist to express what he saw as our proclivity toward what would soon become an obsession with brands and celebrity. Twyla Tharp, who famously choreographed "Little Deuce Coupe" by The Beach Boys for the Joffrey Ballet, created the first "crossover ballet"—a mix of ballet, modern dance, and pop music. No one had seen dancers move like that before. John Cage, one of the most influential composers of the twentieth century and a leading figure in the postwar avant-garde movement—turned music on its ear when he pioneered electroacoustic music and nonstandard use of musical instruments. He was known to have said, "I can't understand why people are frightened by new ideas. I'm frightened of the old ones."

These artists broke form. They *intended* to discover and express *new* things. In fact, this is what artists sign up for: advancing civilization by seeking new forms, new ideas, new possibilities.

To do so, an artist must embrace the discomfort of *not knowing*. Not knowing is inherently terrifying. It feels like you might die. The idea that one would seek out that state of mind for any reason feels counterintuitive. Because of the discomfort, we tend to grab at our first solutions just to escape *not* knowing. Letting go of *knowing* is like letting go of an addiction.

When an *artist* decides to open up, trust, and suspend what they know—in order to explore what they *don't*—they discover choices. When a *person* embraces this journey, they discover possibilities they never dreamed of before.

I tell my students, "Don't be in such a rush to know! Ask yourselves, what else could it be? And again—what else? Keep asking until something arrives in you that makes your heart beat a little faster."

Once you *think* you *know*, you're done learning. Once you think you know, a door closes. Once you think you know, there is no more discovery. Once we file something away under "Oh, I know that," a space closes.

When we *think* we know something, we stop looking at it. You pass by a tree you've passed by every day for the last year, and you don't even *see* her. You don't see her summon the breeze to lift her leaves and wave at you. You don't see her changing color every day or the family of sparrows she's housing at the very top of her branches. You don't see her dispatch one perfect leaf your way—a gift she has presented just for you.

All that *space* available to open between you and that magnificent tree is left closed when you walk by without *seeing* her. Caught up in all that important *thinking,* no doubt! Thinking about all the stuff you know.

Knowing You Know

Other people constantly bombard us with their descriptions of the world—teachers, preachers, parents, and friends, to say nothing of a 24/7, all-consuming media showering us with opinions. When we allow ourselves to conform mindlessly to someone else's dogma, we fall asleep in the matrix of an *agreed-upon* reality—rather than discovering what is true for ourselves by honoring our own inner perceptions.

When you *know* that you know, you *feel* it.

The question becomes *how* to encourage these feelings of intuition, instinct, awareness, impulse, insight, and clairvoyance. How do we cultivate *knowing*?

The answer is: we quiet the mind to hear our hunches better. It is in stillness that we discover the vastness of who we are beyond our obsessive thinking. It is in stillness that we *experience* ourselves as a presence—the energetic being who crafted the personality in order to play the game of life.

We are much, much more than our thinking, and we are just now waking up to who and what we are beyond the confines of our personality.

When we release our thinking and expand into the present moment without all the mental chatter, we enter a space where the soul can speak.

Thinking and Being—Finding Balance

As I shared with you in Chapter 1, I came to meditation late in life, and I *thought* I was terrible at it! I had such a busy mind. I loved thinking. My entire self-esteem was wrapped up in how clever I thought my mind was.

When I first started, I would sit on my cushion in my ceremonial space and maybe light a candle or some incense. Maybe listen to some Tibetan bells or Gregorian chants. I'd close my eyes and focus on my breath. I was lucky if I could score mere seconds without a thought— that stillness in the "gap," as they say—and that situation went on for years.

Sometimes, I'd be lost in thought for I don't know how long, and then I'd "wake up"—realizing I'd strayed from my original intention—and refocus on my breath.

After practicing for a while, I began to unearth the whispers of a long-standing inner monologue that was utterly toxic. I criticized myself for being bad at meditation: *I thought too much, my thoughts were too negative, I didn't meditate long enough, I wasn't committed enough—I'd never been committed enough. Basically, nothing I'd ever done was good enough.*

After unearthing this stream of self-denigration, I suddenly realized there is no *wrong* way to meditate. This *was* the process: *Attention on breath. Note thoughts without judging them. Accept. Let go. Return attention to breath.* The path to enlightenment does not include beating yourself up for every crappy thought you have.

After a while, I began to crave that blissful communion with air. I realized that every time I returned from thought to breath, I was flexing a muscle. I was being mindful of *when* I was thinking, how much I was thinking, and what I was thinking, and I was *mindfully* refocusing my attention on the present.

As Zen Master Thich Nhat Hanh says:

> I breathe in—I know that I am breathing in.
>
> I breathe out—I know that I am breathing out.

That's it. That's the start of a practice. Before long, you become aware of your *thinking* throughout the day. Before long, you enjoy bringing yourself to the vastness of the present moment in one blessed breath—being there, observing, discovering. Before long, you begin to restore balance.

Meditation creates space between YOU and your *thinking*—and in that gap, magic happens.

Exercise:
Standing Up for Your Own Truth

Here's an exercise you might enjoy.

Close your eyes, and breathe into your heart.

Inhale deeply: I breathe in truth.

Exhale: I breathe out that which no longer serves me.

When your mind wanders, note the quality of your thoughts. Is it planning, judging, worrying, dreaming, working, rehearsing? Just take note and go back to your breath.

There is no right or wrong, no better or worse. There is being mindful of breath, mindful of thoughts, and returning home to breath. That's all.

After ten minutes, open your eyes. When you're ready, open your journal and write:

- Remember a time when you gave up what you knew to be true.

  * Write about how it made you feel.

  * Write about what you learned from the experience.

- Now think about a time you stood by what you knew to be true.

* Write about how it felt, including the sensations—I remember my heart beating fast and the smell of gardenias in the air.

* Write about what you learned from the experience.

Trust in your bones. Cultivate your intuition. Believe in your gut—because that brand of inner knowledge vibrates in our hearts at a particularly powerful frequency.

CHAPTER 3

A Touch of Grace

"I have found the best way to give advice to your children is
to find out what they want and then advise them to do it."
—HARRY S. TRUMAN

I HAVE A PICTURE OF GRACIE, A KEEPSAKE, TAKEN IN NEW HOPE ON THE
first day she came to work. She's wearing a T-shirt with a giant
clock on the front that reads, "Time for Love."

She was seventeen when she started. My brother, David, was six.
And I was just two. She worked at the house two days a week for
five years. Gracie is the touchstone of my childhood; she is the
heart and soul of my earliest memories.

I didn't have much sense of my own mother. She seemed sad and
lonely and not much interested in her children. But Gracie—when
Gracie arrived for work, it was as if a light entered the room. She
talked to us while she cleaned, she talked to us while she cooked,
she hugged us when she came and went, and she wiped away our
tears with love and compassion. Best of all, she made us laugh!
David and I laughed until we fell down with Gracie.

Gracie was, and still is, my standard for what it is to be a first-class
human being.

Somewhere in my fifth year, I developed what some might call an obsessive behavior of sorts. I'd kind of freeze. For instance, I'd stop on a dime and gaze at the cracks in the sidewalk, wondering what they were all about. I'd get stuck on which pair of underpants I should wear that day. I'd stand at the top of the stairs and stare down, unable to muster the courage to descend because *anything* could happen on the way down those stairs and who knew what was at the bottom? My mother called it "raging imagination."

Gracie noticed this as I was getting dressed one day. I was frozen with my hairbrush in hand, gazing into the mirror. To me, it felt like a pause in the construct of time. It felt oddly peaceful, like a daydream without a story. Then, I heard Gracie whisper into the space. "It's okay. Move ahead now," she said. "Let's count off."

"Say, 'One,'" she gently commanded. It worked. I started counting the strokes of the brush through my hair. Somewhere between three and five, I came out of the trance.

It happened once while I was practicing the alphabet. I looked at the long list of letters neatly lined up in a row and thought, *What's all this about again?* They suddenly looked like a secret code—a trap I wasn't sure I wanted to be a part of.

"Count off, darlin'," I heard Grace call out, clear as a bell. "One…" she started.

One…I thought as I wrote the first letter. *Two*…and I wrote the second. It was a perfect technique to get through something by moving forward one step at a time. Count off—move through. Great lesson.

First Place

The best part of summer was the club where David and I learned to swim. The Aqua Club had a Disneyland-sized pool with two diving boards. One of them was a high dive, 9.8 feet straight up—the highest, scariest diving board in the world.

My brother and I were particularly good swimmers. David had won several medals in the Fourth of July races that day, including a silly race that involved taking an egg from one side of the pool to the other using a spoon. While others scooped and splashed, David put the handle of the spoon between his teeth, laid the egg gently in the bowl, and then gracefully breaststroked his way across the entire length of the pool. It was thrilling to watch. He was beautiful with his platinum-blonde buzz cut, steel-blue eyes, and summer-browned skin.

I had also won a race that day, which was all the more special because I was the youngest in the heat. I'm not sure why David and I excelled at swimming so much. Maybe because we lived between a canal and the Delaware River—and our parents didn't want us to drown.

What I wanted more than anything in the world that summer, our last summer before we moved to New York, was to pass the Advanced Beginners Swim Test and go down in history as the youngest kid ever to receive the Advanced Beginners *badge*!

I'd already tried twice to pass this test. I could swim freestyle, backstroke, breaststroke, and side stroke. I could rotary breathe *and* scissor kick—I could even dive off the side of the pool, which I didn't much like. But the *last* requirement to get the much-coveted patch was treading water…and it was my undoing. One minute, YES! Three minutes, I'd drown.

There were a lot of swim teachers trying to help me. "All you have to do is tread water this time," they said. "No swimming, you passed that part already—just treading." They thought they were giving me a break because I wouldn't be tired from the swimming parts of the test. They let me know they were rooting for me, but this was it: my third and *last* attempt at treading water for three minutes.

Drumroll...

I failed. My seven-year-old muscles just weren't strong enough to keep my head above water for that long. Everyone felt bad. It was awkward and sad. I found a willow to sit under. She soothed my disgrace.

Toward the end of the day, my brother, my teacher, and a couple of lifeguards wandered over in a group to talk to me. Gaining the attention of that many big kids was pretty unusual for a seven-year-old. I have to say, I didn't completely trust them. What did they want? It was a trick, right? I didn't think they were going to shame me, but what the heck? I felt bad enough.

Before I knew it, my brother and the others were pressuring me to go off the high dive. *What a stupid idea*, I thought. *I'm just a kid, and I haven't even gone off the low dive!* "You don't have to dive— just jump," they said (as if they could hear my thoughts).

"You can earn your badge," they taunted.

Do you know how many steps UP you have to take to get to the top of a high dive? Me either, but it was way, *way* too many steps straight up. I clung to the rails because I couldn't feel my feet. There were teenagers gathered below, cheering me on. I was about half-way up when I first looked down—*all* the way down. The ground looked a million miles away.

"You're doing great! You're almost there! Go, go, go..." was all I heard from below.

My heart was pounding so hard, I disconnected from the Earth altogether and froze. *What have I done? This was a monumentally stupid idea.* Suddenly, I realized I didn't care what any of them thought. I couldn't go any farther up; I just couldn't do it. But I couldn't go down, either. I felt trapped. The idea of going up *or* down made me want to faint. But I also couldn't just stay where I was! I wanted to give up. I just didn't know how.

I looked at my hand, stuck to the handrail like it was frozen in ice. I could see a tiny version of *me* mirrored back in the silver railing. It looked like a whole other world in there, and I wondered if I could crawl in.

A bird called out, inviting me to fly away. My hand gripped the guardrail harder. *Look up,* I heard from somewhere inside me. It sounded like Gracie.

I did as I was told. I could see the platform above me, maybe seven steps up. It was horribly empty—waiting. Waiting for me. I started to cry. From inside me, I heard, *Come on, Jocie—say,* "One..."

"ONE!" I said and took a step.

Good! Did I *hear* that—or *feel* that acknowledgment?

"TWO..." I took another.

Three. Four. Five. I made it! *Oh, my God! I'm on top of the world!*

"JUMP, JOCIE! JUMP..." I could hear the voices shouting from far below.

Jump?! Are you crazy? Again, I weighed my options: Go back down? One thousand steps backward—no, thank you. *Oh, dear lord, I'm going to have to jump off this board!*

I got on all fours—maybe I could crawl off the thing.

"NOOOOOOO!" came the immediate response from the gallery of fools below—it terrified me! I flattened my belly against the board, clinging to the sides for dear life. *What do you mean, NO?!* I thought.

There, in front of my eyes, minding her own business, was a lady-bug—all red, white, and black of her!

"What are you doing up here?!" I asked.

"JUMP!" I heard again, in the distance. But my eyes were on the ladybug—now in *super* focus.

I pressed my belly into the board.

Forget about them, I heard, in my head. *Look at where you are. Look at where you've brought yourself!* Suddenly, I realized this wasn't about passing or failing—this was about *me* and how far I had come. *Stand up!* came the voice inside.

Just then, the ladybug opened her wings and took off! I watched until she disappeared.

I don't know how long it took me to stand. It felt like a long, *long* trip to the end of the board. I pretended I was an expert diver, so I wouldn't feel like I was walking the plank. Head held high, I walked with as much grace as I could muster, one foot in front of the other, counting all the way. One…two…all the way to the end.

Perched at the edge, I could hear and feel the breeze, much as the ladybug must have. Opening my wings, I leaned forward—and flew into the abyss.

I hit the water with my shins at ninety degrees. Ouch! Down, down, down to the bottom of the deep, deep pool—fingers clutching to my nose. I pushed off *hard* from the bottom—then up, up, up to the surface, kicking wildly for my life.

I broke the surface and gasped for air. I heard my brother yelling, "Jocie, are you alright?" I nodded as best I could. Somehow, I had ascended from the depths without dying.

I swam to the side of the pool, collecting my dignity along the way. There were lifeguards everywhere, making sure I didn't drown. People were leaning over the side—congratulating me. My brother reached down, grabbed my wrist, and pulled me out of the water. "Great going, Sis!" he yammered, as he put his arm around me. I could tell he was proud.

My whole body hurt. My shins were on fire. I looked up at the board where I had been—it seemed impossibly high, but I had done it! Kids and swim teachers gathered around—I had never been celebrated like that before. But the personal victory was far more satisfying than all the sudden attention.

Later that day, they awarded me the thing I wanted most in the world: the *official* Advanced Beginners swim patch—making me the only seven-year-old in the history of the world to have accomplished that feat. I felt as if the sun herself were pinning a first-place medal on me. It was a perfect end to my last weekend in New Hope.

Little did I know it was the end of early childhood as well. The end of innocence. Seven years down, and the next seven would prove to be rocky.

The Power of Seven

Seven is a big number. There are seven days of the week, seven wonders of the world, seven chakras, and seven digits in a phone number (not including the area code), and if you ask 1,000 people what their favorite number is—seven will come up far more often than any other. The seventh son of a seventh son is said to have magical powers; Snow White had seven dwarfs; there's rumored to be a seven-year itch, and if you hit the three sevens on a slot machine, you get a big payoff!

It's often said that every seven years, you become a new person because all the cells in your body have been replaced. Maybe that's true. Certainly, the body has a mind of its own. But what I do believe is this: our souls are evolving, we are on a quest to discover who and what we are, and at this time in our evolutionary journey, we do so by overcoming challenges. I also see that ages seven, fourteen, and twenty-one are major turning points in our journey towards adulthood—and in that regard, I was about to enter an age when I would walk forward without the love and support of the one person I could count on: Gracie.

I didn't believe I could survive without her love—that is, until I was rescued by my love for trees.

Breathing with Trees

Gracie gently pulled my arms from around her waist and eased me into the backseat of the car as I tried to hold it together. Leaning in through the window, she stroked my hair. I drank in her touch. It made me cry. My people didn't touch much. All I knew was I didn't want a life without Gracie. She was my rock, my champion. She pointed me in the direction of my soul and made herself an example of loving kindness.

"You'll be okay, child," she said. "Remember how *strong* you are?" She touched the Advanced Beginner swim patch I had safety-pinned to my seersucker shirt. "You climb mountains," she said, referring to the high-dive challenge.

By the time my mother pulled the car away, I was sobbing. Watching Gracie get smaller and smaller out the back window of the car was like watching the end of a sad movie.

We left New Hope in the early morning. By the time we got to New York, the sun was straight up and scorching hot. As the grown-ups set about moving into the new house, my brother found his room, pulled a book from his backpack, and disappeared into *The Yearling*. I immediately went to the backyard to explore the property.

I found my new mother, who just happened to be a tree, sat down with my back against her, and looked out over the Hudson River. Tree, as I now called her, had limbs and leaves forming a parasol above, protecting me from the hot July sun. A welcome breeze blew in and played leafy songs with my new mother-tree, and I lay back in the grass and fell asleep under her big black arms dressed in soft petal leaves, breezing. My heart filled with love and I dreamed of what my life could be.

"JOCIE…" I sat up. Someone from another world was calling my name.

My mother came out on the terrace and found me up the hill, sprawled out under Tree. "Jocie, come say goodbye to your father—he's leaving for the theatre."

A Meditation Exercise:
Communing with Trees

Here's a lovely way to breathe with trees, just as I learned to do that day as a child.

Go to the park or woods. Find a tall tree with beautiful limbs and leaves. Stretch out on the ground and feel Earth beneath you. Allow yourself to fall in. Feel the roots of the tree catch you and cradle you in her arms. Breathe in the sky. See if you can feel at one with both. Sky above, Earth below. Spend some time here.

Look up through the branches. Observe and take in the beauty of the tree's limbs. Discover what you've never seen before. Is that a squirrel up there on the left bough having lunch?

Look at the space between the branches—between leaves. Look at the space between the forms—without the space between forms, there would be no form.

Inhale deeply.

Pick up a leaf, stone, or blade of grass:

- How does it feel?

- How does it smell?

- *Discover* five things about it.

Check in with yourself. Are you thinking? If so, note "thinking" and refocus on the meditation:

- What is the temperature outside? Feel it.

- Is there any wind?

- What are the sounds?

- Listen to the sounds between bird calls.

- Listen to the sounds between sounds.

When you return home, write about the experience in your journal. What did you discover?

Count with Me

Decades after saying goodbye to Gracie—after becoming a parent myself, after my daughter's seventh birthday—I was awakened at 4:30 in the morning by the roar of what sounded like a train crashing into the house. I bolted up and looked at my daughter curled up next to me, the bed violently rocking beneath us.

"Wake up, Sammy," I said, trying to shake her awake. "WAKE UP, LOVE!" I tried again as the room shook.

Her eyes shot open and locked into mine. "Earthquake…" I whispered through the roar, not wanting to disturb the intruder further.

"Are we going to die?" she asked, without moving a muscle—no emotion at all.

I felt the violence in the space around us as best I could. "No," I said—but inside, I felt we were on the edge. If it were *any* more intense, I couldn't have answered that way.

After the initial twenty seconds of terror quieted, I felt my mind take off—where *was* the designated place to go? The threshold of a doorway is a joke—doors swing violently during earthquakes. That's terrible advice. Oh boy, why hadn't we figured this out? We lived in California for crying out loud.

The electricity had blown, leaving us in blackness, but I could see perfectly. Some *other* kind of vision had set in. The TV lay face down on the floor with shattered glass and other fallen objects around it. The aftershocks started. The pictures on the walls were screaming to escape—one flew past my head.

Get out of the bedroom! I heard, clear as a bell. Some other kind of hearing had set in as well.

I saw a clear path from the bottom of the bed, out the door, to the top of the stairs. Gathering Sammy up—arms around neck, legs around waist—we made it out of the bedroom. My legs were like jelly.

Miles was in Vancouver, directing. Samantha, thank God, had asked to sleep in Mama's bed that night. As I got to the stairs, I saw the terror in my daughter's eyes and sat down on the top step.

"Breathe..." I said, as the house shook with an endless assault of aftershocks. We took one long, slow breath together, and then another.

"Count off, Sammy, count off with me, love. ONE..." I said, and I scooched my butt down the first step.

"TWO," Samantha said as we managed the second.

"Three…four…five…" we counted together as we plopped down the stairs, one by one.

We got to the bottom, and I realized we were in the safest place. I turned my back to the wall and braced my feet against the railing. "You good?" I asked as I stroked her sweet head. She nodded back with a little smile.

I felt I'd come full circle; I was parenting Samantha using the same loving touch I'd been graced with. Thank you, Gracie, for teaching me how to get through, how to be kind to others, and how to love.

We learn by example. We change by decision. We move forward with intention.

CHAPTER 4

Learning to Notice
What *Is*

"All artists, whether they know it or not create from a place
of inner stillness, a place of no mind."

—ECKHART TOLLE

THE MOVE FROM NEW HOPE TO SNEDENS LANDING PROVED CHALLENGING
for me as I struggled to process my first impressions of the place.

Church bells rang out from up the hill fifteen minutes before Sunday
services. Such a lovely invitation to head out and congregate—if
only we went to church.

Throughout the week, groups of children of all ages chased each
other on bicycles and beat down shortcuts through the woods that
connected everyone's properties. They had little regard for boundaries or privacy, which disturbed my mother, who liked to sunbathe
nude with her trusty reflector bouncing UVA rays off her face.

No one locked their doors. Children I barely knew would walk into
the house, beg for a drink, open the fridge, or hang out and cook
with my mother.

In June, flocks of wild turkeys proudly paraded their chicks before our cat, named Mouse, who hunkered—waiting for the opportunity to gobble one up.

Copperheads slithered under rocks, and the men talked of hunting them down, chopping off their heads, and tossing them in the river.

Due to swampland that lay deep in the woods, Snedens has mosquitos the size of golf balls—and I have the kind of blood, or scent, that left me covered in welts (an unfortunate side effect of wandering the woods).

The sound of trains across the river struck me as romantic, and I sometimes felt like I was living in a novel. There was even a Shetland pony named Dobbin, who—led by the "big kids"—carried small children, blindfolded, deep into the woods, in some kind of scary but magical initiation rite.

Snedens, otherwise known as the Landing, is an enclave of houses with personalities as unique as the people who live in them. All around you, you can feel history and generation after generation of intrigue, sex, and an age-old dedication to magic-making.

There were maybe seventy houses when we arrived—*all* of them with children. Whereas in New Hope, I had Peter Daily, my *only* friend, this place had scads of kids. Clusters of them. Packs. Cliques! Kids of all ages met up at various spots along the narrow country road that winds its way down to the river.

To be honest, the place terrified me. These kids, whose parents were mostly artists, had personalities the likes of which you'd find in books like *Wuthering Heights* and *Lord of the Flies*. I kept as low a profile as possible as I tried to figure out the lay of the land.

The place itself is a power spot, meaning the energy swirling about it happens to have a little extra *something*. Some energy vortexes are well-known wonders like Stonehenge and The Great Pyramids of Giza, while others are scattered around the world in places like Sedona, in Arizona; Mount Fuji, in Japan; or the Ojai Valley, in California, where I would spend the better part of a year in boarding school. One of the ways you know you're experiencing a power spot is *everything* gets amplified.

Not only could I *feel* the magnified energy coming from that little alcove of history, the social scene was amplified as well. As far as the adults were concerned, let's just say there was a lot of sleeping around. And for their children, wild as the honeysuckle that grew along the roadside in summer, life was BIG, sensual, and dramatic—and for me, overwhelming.

All said and done, Snedens has an undeniable enchantment about it and plays an important role in the landscape of my early memories.

In those first few post-Gracie years, I looked for friends but found no one I could trust or count on. Instead, I experienced all the usual growing-up encounters of friendship and betrayal, love and cruelty, loneliness, loss, and longing.

In Snedens, I shifted from a child with the courage to run bridges and climb towering diving boards to an introverted, questioning, watching, worrying, wondering child—one who longed to be loved and hungered to make a life of her own.

These were the years I discovered I had invisible friends—angels, guides, and an inner voice that served as due north when I went searching for the truth—or my soul.

These were the years I learned to calculate the behaviors of those around me as if my life depended on it.

These were the years I learned the safest way forward was to stand on the sidelines and take it all in—to *observe*.

The Power of Objective Observation

Objectivity is the ability to *perceive* something—as it is—without being influenced by personal emotions or prejudices. It is born of the ability to observe a thing or situation while suspending fixed ideas.

- Open, objective observation of life is the artist's greatest friend.

- It allows us to look at what we *think* we know and discover what we *haven't* seen.

- It allows us to enter the *now*—just as an actor seeks to enter the *moment.*

- It allows artists to *not know*, by choice—in order to discover.

I ask actors and directors in class to observe lots of things, starting with their own behaviors—their routine tasks throughout the day, walks in nature, and habitual ways of thinking, moving, and talking—and then *other* people's habitual ways of thinking, moving, and talking. Much of an artist's time might best be spent simply *observing*.

Artists live to discover. In order to discover, you have to *be* in the present moment and *look*. Look, witness, observe, watch, listen, learn, see—the practice of open, objective observation, of even the most mundane rhythms in life, is how we learn to live in the *now*.

Observing without judgment creates a space for inspiration to arrive. A place to come to your own sensibilities.

Sometimes, arriving in this space requires you to surrender. In stillness, you *invite* the power of NOW to enter. It's as if you open to the energetic vitalities *outside* your body—and summon those forces to merge with the energetic presence that is YOU *inside* your physical form.

Everything is made up of energy. Acknowledging energies outside our body will enhance our connection to the energetic, spirited self inside.

You can't get there with words, or thinking, or *mind*—instead, you *open* to the concept and *feel* yourself expanding. It's visceral. Objective observation is a tool for living in the moment.

My mother, at the end of her years, could go apoplectic over carrots. *I wasn't cutting them correctly! They were too big! She paid for organic, and these definitely were not! Did the grocer, who delivered the order, really think she was the kind of person who would eat this shit? What an insult! What an outrage!*

Often, I would judge her. I'd resent her inclinations toward drama, feeling she spewed her pent-up rage without any regard for the effect she had on others. Negative splatter is infectious. Emotional dramatization spreads itself like disease—like a virus of the soul.

And then, one morning, as my mother was pitching a fit about the size of the eggs she was cracking, I decided to just observe her without engaging in our emotional history.

Because meditation had helped me observe with interest, as opposed to judgment, I was able to let go of my habitual way of engaging in the relationship. In so doing, my ego disengaged, and my need to judge her slipped away.

In the brand-new space created by objective observation, I suddenly saw that it wasn't *my* mother misbehaving; it was an older woman in distress. I saw for the first time that my mother was kicking up all that drama because the sensations of anger made her feel more *alive*. She was using powerful negative emotions as fuel because it was readily available, and she didn't know how to conjure energy in any other way.

Once I saw this, I realized it wasn't uncommon—particularly with the elderly. Once I observed her objectively—*not* from my emotional habits, but from that space I'd created with my breath—the scene unfolding conjured compassion as opposed to contempt.

Objective observation of the present moment quiets the mind and expands our capacity for honest interest in all things outside ourselves. It's how we learn. It's how we discover our own point of view as opposed to being shown or told what to think by others.

When we practice putting aside what we *think* we know, in order to *observe* objectively, we create space for that which we have *yet* to learn. Often, we see things in a totally new way.

Children Are Natural Artists

My daughter, Samantha, has been observing life from her own point of view since she was a small girl. She just *sees* things differently. Children often do. As a kid, my daughter expressed her discoveries in drawings. I would give her a journal when we traveled, and as much as she would write in it, she also liked to draw pictures of her experiences.

One time while we were visiting my mother in Snedens, a wonderful artist I know, Edward, wanted to take Sam to the city on an adventure. She was six years old. Edward was eccentric. I was a protective mom. I would never have considered it if it weren't for his wife, Noriko—a beautiful, serene, and very sane Japanese woman who would be holding Samantha's hand. But mostly, I said yes because Sammy really wanted to go. I could tell she wanted to flex her independence.

They were late on their return, which made me very uncomfortable—welcome to parenting. But when she finally arrived, tired and full, she told me with great excitement they had gone to at least four pizza parlors in a contest for the best slice. It was a perfect outing—she had a wonderful time.

The next day, she drew a picture in her journal. Three people at a four-top, in a pizza parlor—a small girl eating pizza with a couple. What surprised me about the picture was her point of view: it was from the ceiling looking down. Round tops of heads, round tables, round plates, round pizzas with triangle slices. She *sees* things her own way and expresses that discovery. That's an artist. Simple.

A month or so later came a picture she'd made of a basketball game she'd gone to with a friend. It was also from an aerial viewpoint, although not straight down this time. She had drawn the arched windows of the gymnasium, which also served as the school's chapel, and as the four o'clock light streamed through the church windows, she had included lines of *energy* coming through the windows—light. What further amazed me was several of the players she had drawn were half off the page. When I asked her about it, she told me they were either arriving from places we could not see or departing for places we cannot know.

At this point, I thought a good parent would find a place where the kid could explore her talent. I took her to a renowned art school for children, where she gamely spent her weekends that summer, listening to and applying their lessons.

About five weeks in, she sat down at the dinner table and announced she needed a family powwow. She laid out her drawings from class—lovely renditions of classic impressionism, her version of well-known van Gogh, Matisse, Monet, and Renoir—and said, "Guys, why am I going to this school to learn how to art? I already know how to art."

She was six. She was right:

- Being an artist is a state of mind. It is the practice of personal viewpoint.

- Being an artist is the quest for freedom from every-thing but your own discovered point of view.

- Being an artist means looking at the world from a certain place within yourself—a sacred place of nonjudgment—and then expressing your discovered truths.

Bonus Exercise:
Drawing the Unknown

We all have patterns we'd do well to shake. In the ways we walk, talk, look at, and think about things. Too often, we're on automatic pilot, asleep at the wheel. As such, we go through life missing all the best bits—like our own point of view.

If you've ever studied drawing, you'll know there are exercises designed to engage the right side of the brain, the creative side, in order to open yourself up to new possibilities.

Here are three basic drawing exercises—Drawing 101, if you will. Please have fun with them; they will wake you up to new ways of looking at things.

- What is meant by negative space?

    * Place your hand on a piece of paper. With a soft pencil or crayon, shade the entire area around your hand.

    * Lift your hand. Everywhere you see shading is the *negative* space. Most of the time, we take in life through forms—people, places, and things. Focusing on the *negative* space, which is literally the *space* around forms, opens up possibilities. That space holds a power—it holds light. Without that space, *nothing* would exist.

    * Finish your drawing by filling in the form of your hand in any way you like.

- Blind contour drawing

  * Pick an object. It could be a shoe, a corkscrew, or a pair of scissors—something that would fit on your page. Put the object in front of you.

  * You are going to slowly draw the outline of the form without lifting your pencil and without looking at the paper! Draw one long, continuous line as carefully as you can, looking only at the contour of the object. Capture every edge, crack, and cranny possible.

  * Once you've captured the entire outline of the form, keep your pencil on the page, but move it into the inside spaces, drawing the outline of them as well, without looking at the page. The inside of the scissor handle, the outline of the screw. The tongue of the sneaker and its laces. Remember not to lift the pencil. This exercise calls for trust.

  * When you are done, look at your page. Cool huh? Don't judge. Remember, there is no right or wrong in art.

- Drawing the negative space

  * Pick a ladder-back chair, a stool, or a vase of flowers for this one—something that has well-defined negative spaces when you look at it.

* Drawing the negative shape demands a whole new way of *seeing*. You need to forget the object—you are not drawing it. This is the opposite of contour drawing. You're going to observe the shapes of the spaces in and around the object—and draw those. From the edge of the page to where it meets the object: the drawing starts there. This perspective can be a bit dizzying as you take in a new reality.

* See the spaces, then draw them, trusting that the negative will define the positive. The positive form is left undrawn but arrives—like magic—as you create the space around it. The positive does not exist without the negative and vice versa.

These are all exercises to help you open up your perspective. They help you see in a different sort of way. They help you discover what you didn't see before.

Instead of drawing what you think you see, these exercises will keep you in the present, engage your trust, and open you to new possibilities.

If you find yourself judging your drawings, simply take note, and go back to drawing. We're playing here. The spirit of play is important. Playing is freedom. There is no right or wrong in art.

Teaching Objective Observation
to Actors on Stage

In order to bring an actor to the present moment, I will sometimes prompt them to observe things as they're playing the scene. For instance, if an actor is disconnected, self-conscious, or *showing* us how they think it should go, I'll focus their attention by saying something like:

> Don't worry, just look at the table.

> Really look.

> Note the color.

> Feel the texture.

> Take your time.

> Find an imperfection you've never seen before.

> Now…caress the table as if it's the back of a baby you love.

> Say your lines to the table as if you're talking to the baby.

I want to direct the actor's attention so they can experience *being* in the moment while juggling more than one thing. I might say:

> Feel the coffee cup in your hand.

> Where did it come from?

How long have you had it?

Take a sip.

Feel the heat of the ceramic against your lips.

Think about what happened last night.

Say the line.

An actor has to *arrive* in the moment in order to *enter* the scene in a truthful way. It helps to focus their attention before they rush ahead with the words.

It takes courage to simply *be*. We're afraid we're not interesting enough; plus, we feel exposed when we respond in a simple, clear, and honest way. To *be* in the moment, you must slow down and focus your attention.

Easing an actor's attention off themselves and on to objective observation is a fine way to teach them to rub their belly and pat their head at the same time. Acting is juggling lots of different things at the same time—just as we do in life. The idea is for the actor to *experience* their sensory gifts *in the moment*. I want actors to:

- See, hear, taste, touch, and feel—while they're acting

- Experience real thoughts and feelings

- Trust that they're enough

- Behave as real people

- Notice when they're judging and change course

I want these things for everyone.

Once the actor knows they're connected—then and only *then* should the words come. This is how to make the lines improvisational:

- A person doesn't know what they're going to say

- An actor doesn't know how they're going to say it

Observing the present *while* you're acting builds trust in the coordination actors must learn. Real observation, real thoughts, real feelings, and focused behavior—*before* the words. That's the practice. Like juggling.

I want actors to practice juggling lots of choices, in lots of scenes, until they *own* that coordination. Until being in the moment becomes as effortless as riding a bike. Once they have certainty about their technique, their choices will deepen and mature. True for acting, true for life.

Do you see how this applies to all of us? *Being* in the moment, taking in what's around us, listening before we speak—as opposed to entertaining our own ego with chatter designed to capture interest and impress. People who *try* to be interesting are inevitably a bore. Interesting people are the ones most *interested* in things outside themselves.

I remember a young girl in my class, maybe twenty years old, doing a love scene with a gorgeous French boy a little older than she. Her shyness was palpable. It seemed painful for her to be on stage, much less expose her real feelings for the young man in front of her. I wanted to bring her to the moment and, at the same time, give her permission to fall in love a little—which was what the scene called for. They were sitting at a café table across from each other. I spoke gently:

Don't worry; just…notice the mole on Michael's neck.

Notice the little blonde hairs around it.

Sense the temperature of his body there.

Say the line…

Can you sense the heat of his skin?

The texture?

His scent?

Take your time.

Think of what it would be like to bury your face in his neck.

Touch your neck in the corresponding place.

Say the line…

Part your lips.

Think of what it'd be like to kiss him?

Ooooops! Too much!

Close them.

Drink from your wine glass quickly, in case he noticed your thoughts.

Don't worry; the blushing is genius—embrace it.

Smile.

Focus your attention on the beauty of the mole.

The mole is everything!

Say the line...

Force yourself to look down at your fork.

Push a piece of celery around the plate slowly.

Listen to Michael speak. Listen hard—is it possible he's saying, "I love you"?

Actors have to connect to *something* other than the words. I tell them, "Good acting is easy. It's just a little difficult trusting in the simplicity. Humanity has long been in the business of complicating things."

A Meditation Exercise:
Objective Observation

Here's a way to practice your newfound understanding of objective observation.

Take ten minutes alone in a place of your choosing. It could be a café, a park, a waiting room, a store, or even your own home.

You are going to focus your attention on simply observing—observing a person, place, animal, or tree.

- Ground yourself with your breath until you have stilled.

- Settle in until *you* are present.

- Take in what's before you. Focus. Give it your full attention. Your attention is a gift.

- If thoughts come up, note them. Are you thinking of the past? The future? Are you passing judgment? Take note and go back to simply observing.

- Stay open.

- Take some time with your senses—what is there to see, hear, taste, touch, or smell?

- Let the names of things drift away.

- Let the labels drift away.

- Let your preconceptions drift away.

- When you feel your objectivity slipping and thoughts flood in again, note their quality. Are you comparing, criticizing, worrying, planning, rehearsing, fantasizing, feeling bored? Boredom is a form of judgment. Accept your thoughts and return to observing.

- After a while, take in the negative space—the space between things—the air between form. Like the air we breathe, there is a powerful energy waiting to be acknowledged and engaged. This is the space of all possibility.

If you feel compelled to talk about these personal experiences with others, take note of it and practice *not* having to say everything that's on your mind. When you keep your spiritual experiences private, a trust builds between you and your higher self.

When you chitchat about that which you find sacred, you diminish the power of your practice. You move out of the high frequency of *experiencing* and return to your personality's desire to impress.

This is the process:

> Look, listen, and expand! Be present as a person, not a critic.
>
> Try not to add anything up.
>
> Just keep looking.
>
> You'll come to conclusions.
>
> Fine.
>
> Keep looking.
>
> You'll come to assumptions.
>
> Okay. What else? Keep looking.
>
> Enter the experience. And let the experience *enter* you.

Objective observation is a technique anyone can use to bring themselves to the moment. The more you practice living in the moment, the more you will enhance your ability to discover your own truth. The more you practice living in the moment, the more you will be able to manifest by co-creating with your higher self.

Observing without judgment is a living, moving meditation. Living with this practice will open your mind and lead you to the calm embrace of your most authentic self—the artist.

CHAPTER 5

Living in the Moment

"The moment you doubt whether you can fly, you cease forever to be able to do it."

—J.M. BARRIE, PETER PAN

AS A YOUNG GIRL, ONE OF MY FAVORITE THINGS TO DO WAS TO "ROCK hop." We lived along the Palisades, a 200-million-year-old rock column towering as high as 500 feet over the Hudson River.

The woods around our home, leading down to the Hudson, have a number of brooks and streams that babble along, happy in their flow—certain in their mission to become one with the river. Many of them are wide enough to have rocks and boulders in their beds that are hundreds of thousands of years old. Each has a personality all its own.

In the spring, the rains arrive, and the snow melts, filling the brooks to capacity, often spilling over and pushing wide the stream. As the water tumbles over the boulders, it polishes them to a smooth and inviting surface. In exchange, the water is *enlivened*. It is an exquisite communication between water, rock, sun—and finally, my feet.

Summer is the best season for rock hopping. In summer, the water runs low, and the stones caress your feet with heat they've soaked up from the sun.

Rock hopping is running up the streams, which make their own natural pathways, leaping surefooted from one rock to another, noting what's in your immediate vicinity—a patch of wild columbine to the left of you, a tail feather some turkey left behind to your right. When I run these rocks, soaking up the magic beneath my feet, I can feel the Algonquin peoples who ran them before me—as if timelines are bleeding.

Creating Life, Moment to Moment

I tell my students this "rock hopping" story to illustrate that moment-to-moment acting is not just *living* in the moment improvisationally. There's another dimension to it. There is *discovering* and creating the moments in your rehearsals—each crafted moment like another rock in the riverbed. You feel free to leap because you trust there is a boulder to land on—it's a solid piece of structure you built. You trust because you created it yourself—it is *personal* to you.

Creating the riverbed is the actor's homework. *Living* in the moments of that structure is the execution, the performance, the improvisation, the *flight*. Two kinds of moments: the created moment and the improvised moment—both equally important.

It is the structures you create in life that lay the groundwork for an exciting existence, one that feels like flying. It's the rock that calls out to the feet.

When you focus your attention and simply *do* the things you do with care, you arrive in the present. When an actor does the same, we *enter* the moment with them because they offer us an alternative reality they *believe* in. When they believe, we believe.

For example, in the movie *Atlantic City*, Susan Sarandon returns home from work as a waitress at an oyster bar. The film creates a wonderful *moment* by revealing her after-work routine. Standing in front of her kitchen window, she languidly squeezes lemons over her nude torso to kill the smell of fish. The writer, director, or actor *created* that moment—and it's a fine piece of behavioral structure that tells an important part of the story without words. We see this is what she does every day when she comes home from work. This is the rock.

How Sarandon enters that behavior is the flight. In this performance, the behavior has a routine about it; she has worked with fish for a while now, and we see she does this every day. But *today*, it has a longing about it—it is sensual. She is thinking about a man, perhaps. Because the man in Sarandon's mind is *personal* to her, we *sense* him there.

Out of the actor's understanding of story comes not only their personal choices for inner life but also their behaviors and *how* they do them. How does a woman knead bread? Okay—how does an *angry* woman knead bread? Once the actor connects to their *personal* choices, the words arrive.

There you have three-dimensional acting: *thoughts and feelings* (inner life), which then color how the actor *does* the *behavior*, and after they connect to all that, the *words* come.

Training actors in this way is like teaching them to juggle. It takes coordination. And, like riding a bike, once you get the hang of it, it's fun!

As another example, in the movie *A Streetcar Named Desire*, a drunken Stanley, played by Marlon Brando, has beaten his pregnant wife, Stella—who escapes with her sister, Blanche, to the neighbor's upstairs apartment. In a moment reminiscent of the *Romeo and Juliet* balcony scene, albeit more pathological, Stanley stands in the courtyard calling up, "Hey, Stella...STELLAAAAA!"

That is the story, and those are the words—they form the *rock*. But it was *how* Brando played Stanley—feeling beside himself, thinking he had gone too far and lost his beloved Stella forever—in other words, it was his *flight* that catapulted him into stardom. It was his commitment to loving someone so deeply he might not survive without that love being returned. Brando took Stanley from a brute to a baby—a baby so deeply in love with his Stella, and no one could resist him! Suddenly, we understood a woman's love for an abusive man.

The humanity Brando found for the character was so astounding that the first time Tennessee Williams saw him in the part, he was compelled to say, "I wrote that?" He thought he had written a Neanderthal! He was deeply moved by the personal choices Brando had found for Stanley.

Actors can explore these kinds of scripted moments, make discoveries, and find an understanding of life in *such* detail that the moments become like carved-out vignettes. These vignettes become as solid for the actor as one of those boulders in my stream. In this way, I encourage actors to enter a balance between the known and the unknown—to fling themselves into the moment with abandon, trusting that they will land on the next rock.

It is the same for anyone consciously creating their own life. The more confident you are in the structural choices you make for your life, the more freedom you'll feel living in the moment. The more freedom you feel living moment to moment, the more joy you invite into your life.

To witness the emancipation of a person's creativity brought about by their confidence in a technique they've made their own—this brings me the greatest joy.

Falling in Love with the Mundane

Even as we learn to consciously create our lives, we have large parts of our day we consider routine and boring. We train ourselves to move through these kinds of behaviors automatically. When we drive, cook, bathe, dress, or do laundry, we go through the motions while *thinking* about other things. We write off our routines as tedious, and if we can multitask, so much the better. We're obsessed with "saving time."

As if we could do that—save time. Man, oh, man! Imagine if we could bank time and use it later like a saving account. Wow! That would be cool. But this is planet Earth, and there is no "saving time." There is only fully experiencing the moment...or not.

Why do we feel compelled to rush through the moment, anyway? And toward *what* exactly? A future that doesn't exist? There is no future! The present moment is the only *real* time we have.

Do you feel like life is going too fast? Do you want to slow it down? Then BE in the moment. The more fully you experience the moment of NOW, the...more...you...slow...down...time.

Time is ripping by because we're not *in* it. This is the essential problem with humankind. Most of the *time*, only the thinnest slice of *us* is actually present and experiencing what *is*.

How do we turn this around? Like many things, it's so simple that it's difficult. I talk to my students about:

- The power of stillness in performance.

- Stilling themselves in order to observe without fixed ideas.

- Stilling themselves as a way to connect to that sacred space wherein their work can be influenced by their most inspired impulses.

I say, "Still yourself, and see how much detail you can observe in the moment. Dare to *be* there. *Being* there expands you because it expands time."

Whether they are observing human behavior or some magnificent display of nature—I tell my students that in order to harness the power of objective observation, they need to slow down, breathe deeply, and take in the *details*. God lives in the details.

Oddly, it is the *mundane* details of life that bring the truth to both acting and living. The first step is to *observe* them—the next step up is to *admire* them. When you fall in love with the mundane details of moment-to-moment living, you fall in love with the miracle that is life.

Say you're a coffee drinker. You have a routine you go through every morning to get to that first yummy, comfortable sip. When we're in the moment, we notice and appreciate every detail:

- We smell the delicious coffee beans.

- We are grateful for easy access to pure water.

- We caress the smoothness of a hand-thrown cup, appreciative of its maker.

- We notice the tiny chip on the handle.

- We feel the coolness of the silver spoon as it slips into the steaming hot liquid.

- And we hear the music as we stir, tapping the spoon against the inside of the cup.

All of this detail is lost when we don't pay attention. Lost when we judge it to be uninteresting. Lost time.

All this *thinking* we do instead of *being* is a contraction. Being in the moment—experiencing the moment in all its fullness—expands us. In fact, it *creates* time.

Being there and discovering your own point of view by observing and admiring the tiniest, most mundane details in life is a technique for coming into your own. Becoming your own person and developing your own point of view is the most relevant thing you can do in both life and art.

Learning to observe and admire the things you've considered boring is a practice that will elevate your perspective. When you're able to direct your own interest by observing routine behavior, you expand your capacity to experience deeper truths about reality. Time belongs to *you* in the now.

Admire the blade of grass. Give it its due. Live from a place of gratitude for the tiny "mundane" miracles in life, and you will find yourself living in the moment—heart full, wide awake, and filled with joy. Like the river seeks the sea, life begins to *flow* in the right direction.

I believe we are evolving from egoic beings who *learn* by creating problems, dramas, and crises to identify with and solve...into awake, energetic beings who *manifest* life by living in the moment, listening for the impulse of divine inspiration, and recognizing the synchronicity that follows as an affirmation that we are on the right path.

The First Exercise

The very first exercise I give actors is about creating an environment. It teaches them how to create a place in which to live. It also teaches them how to elevate the ordinary to the extraordinary. The components of the exercise are as follows:

- Create a familiar environment on stage.

- Be alone in that world.

- Really *do* the things you do by applying careful attention while doing them.

Actors need to create a world to live and behave in it. To help them build this parallel life, I ask them to observe their own behavior. We all have what I call *life rhythms*—routines that make up the structures of our day: waking up in the morning, coming home from work, preparing a meal, getting ready for the day, packing for a trip, cleaning our rooms, shaving, and so on. We typically consider these tasks boring and perform them on automatic pilot as we *think* about other things.

This basic exercise helps actors settle into their *life* on stage. It teaches them to slow down, focus their attention, and *still* themselves in the present moment. It teaches them to *be* there. It is an exercise, a meditation, and a way to rehearse—all in one.

The Environment Exercise

- Observe your life. Look for the daily routines that make up the structures of your day.

- After a few days of observing, choose one of these living vignettes.

- For the next week, observe yourself moving through that daily task and begin to string together your detailed behaviors as an exercise. You will have to become present to accomplish this.

- Rehearse these behaviors, focusing on each as if it were a gift. It is. It's a precious piece of life you've captured, like lightning in a bottle that you will later open and release on stage.

- Rehearse this track of behaviors, knowing they are the same behaviors you will repeat in class. Remember: God lives in the details. Training your focus on this lineup of simple human behavior will ground you in the present and give you a place to listen from.

- Take your time.

- Always look for more detail. The acuity of your focus is everything.

- Always be open to improvising if the spirit moves you.

- Always acknowledge and act on an impulse.

- Always be on the hunt for something you didn't see before.

- Imagine how to create your set.

- Make a list of what you will bring to the stage.

- Choose a few personal items, and endow them with an energy that can be retrieved when you perform— for instance, the red chair you bought with your first boyfriend just before you broke up. Every object has its own role in the play at hand. Every specific piece of behavior is threaded together like pearls on a neck- lace, one pearl after the other, and you are the thread.

- Once the object is empowered, say the red chair, sit on it and imagine being on stage. Practice your depth of focus as you do the behaviors you've strung together for yourself. This is a rehearsal. Rehearse often.

- Review the checklist of props and other things you have chosen to bring to the stage. Make sure you bring every one of them. Make sure you use every one of them. Make sure every one of them returns home at the end of the night by checking them off your list. These objects are your first scene partners—take good care of them.

- The last thing you do before you start your "scene" is to take in the environment you created. Everything you brought to the theatre is there for a reason. You saw it in your mind's eye, and here it is—manifested!

We store bits and pieces of furniture at our theatre to enable actors to build their own sets. We always have a small couch, a bed of some kind, tables, chairs, black boxes, a sink—even a toilet seat on a black box serves as a privy. We give actors the building blocks to form an environment in which to live and play.

The actors then bring in their own personal props to further dress the set and make it their own. Some bedding, kitchenware, laundry to fold, a whistling kettle here, a child's bicycle there—maybe even some Christmas lights or a fan to help believe in the season or temperature.

We have stage managers who help the actors create their set. We provide lights, sounds, and music should they want any or all. We give actors the whole kit and caboodle because it stimulates their imagination and expands their choices. Most importantly, it helps them *believe*.

As they get ready to *live* in their environment on stage, the actor endows everything around them with their belief. *Yes, this is my kitchen counter. This is the hairbrush I use, and here are the pins.*

They have created a place and a behavioral structure with reference points. *This is where I place the mail; after that, I cross the room, sit on the couch, and take off my shoes. Once my tired feet are free, I rub them as I glance through the mail.* Their confidence is high because they've earned their right to *be* their own story. Their behavior is real because they've taken it from their life or imagination and rehearsed it.

The involvement of creating a place, *being* in it, and behaving in real time helps the actor *behave* like a real person. I want actors to respond as people, not "actors." Without the burden of words, they have a fuller sense of being alone in a place and performing tasks in a truthful way. As unglamorous as that sounds, that's acting.

As the actors rehearse their moment-to-moment behavioral structure, they become more confident in the path they created from their life and imagination. The more involved they become with the details on stage, the more *life* they produce. The more life they produce, the more we suspend our reality and take the journey with them.

It is living and loving the mundane moments on stage that earns you the right to take flight in the big ones. It is the plié before the leap that holds the power.

The Environment Exercise in Action

I love actors who come to acting late in life. I find it brave—not only to admit their secret desire out loud but also to do something about it.

For instance, I had a police officer interview for class. He had always dreamed of becoming an actor. On his fiftieth birthday, he decided it was now or never and set up an interview with me.

I asked him if he was a good cop. He said, "Yes."

I asked him, "What makes you a good cop?"

He thought about it before saying, "I give it everything I have because I really care."

I welcomed him to class and told him that was his first lesson: *give all that you have.*

The Environment Exercise was his first time on stage. After observing his daily routines, he decided to recreate the locker room at his police station. Dressing for duty was his daily routine. In this exercise, we saw the world of a police officer suiting up for work. There was vast detail in *how* he dressed, how he put on his pants, shirt, belt, the apparatus hanging off the belt, etc. When he was dressed, he closed the cabinet and turned to leave. He got halfway across the room, stopped, and turned back. Opening the locker again, he looked at a picture he'd taped inside the door. It was a picture of a friend who'd been killed in the line of duty. After taking the photo in, he pulled out a bulletproof vest and slipped that on as well.

This was the life he'd discovered through observation and built into a structure during rehearsal. It was his first time on stage, and I could have filmed him. He was a real person, doing a string of behaviors exactly as he had done hundreds of times in life—and we couldn't take our eyes off him.

In the critique, he said he had no idea he did all those things. He realized if he hadn't focused on the details and had instead continued on automatic pilot, he'd find getting dressed on stage as unimportant as he did in life. He told us he'd experienced the moment with his partner's picture yesterday, and because of his newfound awareness, he knew he wanted to incorporate it into his first exercise on stage.

In an eight-week master class that we filmed, an experienced actress was playing Janice in John Patrick Shanley's *Italian American Reconciliation*. Because she knows this work, she created an environment that reflected what a wreck her character is. Clothes strung all over the place, old plates of crusty food lying about—dead and dying plants—and there she was, sprawled out on an unmade bed, wearing sweats, stuffing her face with eggrolls and spareribs while watching *The Honeymooners* on TV.

None of this was in the script. It was a life fashioned by the actress. A life she created to ground herself in her character. She'd created a mess of an environment because it made her *feel* like the mess of a girl she was playing—and the Chinese food and TV kept her from anticipating the upcoming scene. If the other actor never arrived, and the scheduled scene never took place, she was fully involved in the life of her character—and we could have watched her for hours.

Exercise: Creating *Your* Environment

I am continually struck by the similarities for both actors and everyday people in creating a successful life for themselves.

For instance:

- The ability to create a safe place to live in with confidence

- The ability to be alone and content

- The ability to be present when you do the things you do

- The ability to make choices that forward your life in the direction you wish

- The ability to govern your own emotions and attitude

- The ability to apply focused attention when and where you wish

Here is an exercise that will help you gain more mastery over your environment.

What you wake up to in the morning is important. Remind yourself to spend the first fifteen minutes tomorrow morning sitting up in bed and taking in your environment. Observe the room. If you have a partner there, that's fine—that person is a part of the life you're creating. Take in the details and notice how the space makes you feel.

Then practice this meditation:

Close your eyes and listen to your breath for ten minutes.

Inhale: I breathe in space—I expand.

Exhale: I am grateful for all that is around me.

After ten minutes, open your eyes. When you are ready, open your journal and write about your bedroom:

- What do you love?

- What do you like?

- What don't you like?

- What do you need?

- What don't you need?

- Is there anything you'd like to change?

Have fun imagining what would make the room ideal for you. Envision a room you would love to wake up to, and then:

- Make a list of what you need to realize your vision.

- Spring clean every inch of it.

- Get rid of everything you don't need or love.

- Make space.

- Paint walls if you like.

- Buy, or better yet, make, something new.

- Check things off your list as you accomplish them.

Once you get your bedroom settled, move on to the rest of your home and do the same. Make sure that you have a *sacred space* of your own, if only a corner. Everyone needs a place to be alone with their thoughts to meditate, pray, and imagine in. Make sure your space includes a plant or cut flowers, even if it's only a single daisy. Plants are alive. They bring a spirited vibration to your life. Admiring and caring for living things enlivens spirit.

As you make your place even more your own, you'll find you'll wake up in the morning, admire the details of what you've created, and instantly feel grateful. Gratitude is an effortless way to fall into the practice of being in the moment. Gratitude brings joy.

We respond to the aesthetics of our environment. Where we live and what's around us have a profound effect on how we feel. How we feel determines our vibration. When we create order, cleanliness, and beauty in our surroundings, those qualities harmonize within us.

CHAPTER 6

Finding Spirit

"You do not belong to you. You belong to the universe."
—R. BUCKMINSTER FULLER

MY FIRST DIRECT ENCOUNTER WITH MY OWN INTERNAL GUIDANCE CAME when I was in the third grade. The day before my eighth birthday, I was walking to my new school feeling profoundly sorry for myself. *I just don't understand why they don't see me. I came into this world with gifts to share. I came to offer my heart. I have messages. I came to help!*

It never occurred to me that my parents couldn't see that in me. It never occurred to me that I couldn't awaken joy in them by my mere presence. I was pretty sure my purpose in life was to bring joy, and I felt sad that I was failing in my mission.

Well, Jocie, we're here, and we might just have to be enough, came the answer, clear as a bell.

It's not like I heard the individual words. It's more like the whole concept arrived. In this case, it was pretty matter of fact—kind of like, *We're here. You're blessed. Get over it.*

It came from somewhere inside me—or outside—sometimes it feels like both. I'd always had an easy, ongoing communication with this extra-dimensional world. I was grateful for the support, truly, but I longed for some kind of three-dimensional companion to help me weather this physical-Universe illusion I'd woken up in once again.

It's not like I picture angels flying about, or spirit guides, or entities of any kind—although my whole life, people who *see* that sort of thing have told me I travel with quite a crowd. And it isn't like I hear *actual* voices. It's more like I feel surrounded by an invisible tribe who simply walk with me, protect me, and advise me in a gentle sort of way. Their presence feels as natural to me as breathing, and I have "walked" with them for as long as I can remember.

Because they seemed such an integral part of me, it took a while for me to understand that I could actually "work" with them on different levels.

The first conscious conversation, if you can call it that, came about because I asked a direct question. Playing along the riverbank one day, skipping stones, feeling alone and alienated from pretty much everyone, I asked, "Who can I trust?"

The wind came up and blew the branches of a weeping willow my way. She reached out her long, thin tendril arms to touch my neck. "Us," was the answer. It came in one whole hunk of a concept. I instantly understood that if I wanted to interact with my invisible crew in this third dimension, all I had to do was look to the trees. Well, all of nature really—as nature is the physical expression of spirit, but I didn't know that at the time. I just got *trees.*

It made sense to me because some trees felt more like family to me than my own. Certain trees brought me tremendous solace in those young, tender years. In many ways, it felt like they had raised me— they had certainly tended to my spirit.

As I write about these particular trees, I feel a tremendous reverence fill my heart.

I realize for the first time that every house I have ever lived in has had a mother-tree outside my bedroom window. It's almost as if these trees called me to the place so they could watch over me.

My love affair with trees has been a part of me for as long as I can remember. They're like living angels to me, and I am humbled as I marvel at their presence. How did these giants first come into being? What life force did they possess to push up through the earth and grow into such a powerful, benevolent force—a force that would sustain itself for hundreds, if not thousands, of years. As it is below (oh, those roots), so it is above—the canopies of leaves ever reaching for the sun. How did they know how to *be* so much better than we?

I don't know who I was posing the question to when I asked, *Who can I trust?* If anything, I was talking to myself, there by the river, as we do—not really expecting an answer. But that was the first time an answer arrived from a source I felt I could *communicate* with.

Nature had always moved in me, but now she was speaking to me directly. The willow loomed large, towering and protective as she consorted with the wind. *We love you, Jocie,* she seemed to say. *We are always here for you.*

When spring finally came after a long cold winter, and the flowers exploded, I felt as grateful as I might for the return of a thousand friends. Snow drops and crocus, daffodils and lily of the valley, tulips, peonies, and poppies! And my favorite, bleeding heart—their long, thin stems bowing from the weight of tiny heart-shaped flowers hanging there like earrings. I loved them all. I had a secret language with the flowers, one I didn't share with others.

In the summer, I'd take naps on the rocks of the Palisades overlooking the Hudson. Like a lizard, I'd lie there absorbing the heat they'd soaked up from the sun, waking refreshed from their mineral messages. They have been here forever, after all.

In the winter, when the light of the moon bounced off the snow, illuminating the night, I would ice-skate through the trees on the snow-swept ponds that lay deep in the woods of Snedens Landing.

And when the snow fell straight down in giant puffs, quieting the Earth with its crystalline magic, I would bundle up and take long walks, marveling at the nature of water in all her forms. It's the same water that's been around for five billion years—just recycling itself by evaporating into the heavens and then falling back to Earth in all her many expressions. From mist to hurricane, snow, and hail—it's the same water the dinosaurs were gulping. This astounds me!

I discovered nature to be honest, trustworthy, and a master advisor on all things significant. This is where I direct my most intimate questions and prayers. For me, the planet Gaia is the clearest expression of unity—of God if you like. When in communion with nature, I feel all the many parts come together. I feel whole.

Given that spirit has created nature as such a wondrous reflection of her power to design life, I couldn't understand *how* it was possible for us to ignore her magnificent and paramount communication. How could we take such magic for granted?

Inside my house growing up, complicated egos clashed, and a lack of kindness prevailed. But outside, nature never failed to restore my attachment to spirit. Without that intimate connection within, without her guidance, intuition, and inspiration, I'm not sure I'd be here today.

Finding Home

One night as I addressed my students at the top of class, I felt a heavy energy in the room. I asked them about it and got the regular sort of complaints actors tend to indulge in—not enough auditions, not enough money, not enough time, not enough attention. They seemed weighed down by the smallest of challenges.

I asked them, "When was the last time you spent the day in nature?"

Nothing came back.

"Seriously, when was the last time you went to the beach, or the mountains, or the botanical gardens, or a park?"

They just looked at me.

Nature is a 24/7 example of the miracle that is life. She supplies instant inspiration. She has a way of cutting through the mind and connecting directly to the soul. Nature is home.

So, I gave them an assignment. I asked them to Google "big nature, Los Angeles" and choose a place they might like to spend an hour or so *alone,* in nature, *phone OFF*—simply observing.

Once they arrived at their chosen corner of the world, I told them to take a seat, still themselves, and breathe the place in—absorbing the size and scope of the beauty around them. Look at big things, look at tiny things, and look at the spaces between things. Focus, listen, smell, feel—breathe.

I told them two hours would be good—but very few were able to spend that much time. The youngest said fifteen minutes was enough to blow her mind. She had never *chosen* to spend time in nature, so it was like another realm to her and utterly overwhelming!

The power of nature is intense if you haven't been paying attention and wake up to her suddenly. Start slowly. Follow her lead. To take in all that nature has to offer is to heal yourself. She cleanses. She takes us home to the *now*.

I also asked them to find a rock at some point—"Or better yet, let the rock find you"—and bring it to class as an expression of gratitude for the experience nature offered up that day.

When I walked into the theatre the following week, I saw some fifty rocks lined up on the apron of the stage. The energy in the studio was alive! The actors were buzzing and couldn't wait to tell me about their experiences. The energy shift in the theatre was palpable. Suddenly their problems seemed trivial compared to the abundance of splendor they'd seen around them.

They spoke of overwhelming beauty.

They spoke of feeling at one with the planet.

They spoke of recognizing spirit in trees, birds, flowers, and sky.

They spoke about the power of the ocean and the majesty of mountains.

And they spoke of taking nature for granted, as we do when we're not awake.

One girl was blown away by the fact she gave herself an "entire hour." She had never spent an hour *alone*—period! Not without an electronic device. She couldn't remember *ever* being alone outdoors in the way I was asking. The power of nature was so spirited and alive that it overwhelmed her, and she found herself terrified. But once it was over, like a rollercoaster, she was so wide awake that she wanted to go again. Nature has the power to heal the effects of electronics.

All of them talked about rejuvenation. All felt better about themselves and wanted to incorporate nature into their lives more—or at least make a practice of standing outside to look up—drinking in the sun, moon, stars, clouds, water, wind, and sky.

We took a moment to give thanks. At the end of the class, many of them wanted to give me their rocks. They loaded them into the trunk of my car, and I took them home and incorporated them into my gardens. I have to say, the bulbs were particularly beautiful that year.

We are blessed here in Los Angeles with an abundance of beautiful places to retreat. You can find parks, botanical gardens, beaches, forests, and mountains within a two-hour drive. But wherever you live in the world, you can find retreats and places close by that protect and cultivate nature's beauty.

Whenever you are feeling low and disconnected, you have only to take a walk outside and admire the beauty and power of this planet to revitalize. Nature is vibrating at the highest frequency there is. Inhaling nature will raise your vibration quickly and dramatically.

The Artist's Frequency

After many years of observing actors, this idea came to me out of the blue: an artist is *not* his talent—although, let me tell you, they don't like hearing that much. From my perspective, the artist's gift is not their *talent* but rather their acute *sensitivity*. An artist literally vibrates at a higher frequency, allowing them to pluck impulse out of the ether—universal impulse that is ripe for the times.

Certain things began to make sense to me, like why artists are so often unhappy and why they sometimes feel undeserving. It's because they indulge their egos by believing all the inspiration they're receiving is *them*, when in fact, there's a deeper conversation going on that they're sadly not acknowledging.

Failing to accept such a vital connection is an incomplete communication. They go from the highest vibration—communion with something akin to divinity—to a lower, smaller, self-important vibe. These are two very different frequencies. Diving from one end of the spectrum to the other, as artists do, you're likely to get the bends—yet actors bounce from the high to the low with unhealthy regularity.

I tell my students, "You are never as great as you think you are, and you are never as terrible either. We are all somewhere in the middle. Please stop measuring."

In working with actors these many years, I've discovered that success in acting has little to do with talent. It has first and foremost to do with *desire*, followed by diligence and a positive attitude. Desire, diligence, and a positive attitude all describe a person coming from a place of enthusiasm. If you look up the origins of the word enthusiasm, you'll find it comes from the Greek *en* ("within") + *theos* ("god")—meaning "divinely inspired."

Not only is enthusiasm extremely attractive, it may also be the most *hirable* quality there is! Why? Because people are attracted to the *frequency*! People are drawn to inspired artists because it reminds them that frequency exists inside them, too. In fact, it's their natural state!

So, how do we cultivate a positive attitude? How can we bring more desire, diligence, and enthusiasm to our lives? *Can* we take ourselves from a negative attitude to a positive one in order to raise our frequency at will?

We can if we *choose* to. But we must be *awake* in the moment to make that choice.

Since energy is invisible to the eye, we sometimes have trouble conceiving it as real. Although it can be hard to wrap our minds around, science has long proven that we are made up of energy.

In fact, everything in the Universe consists of energy—all vibrating at different frequencies.

We are energetic beings with an electrical field (frequency) that emanates three feet or more beyond our bodies—proven science. Everything we *think* and *feel* affects our vibrational frequency. *Enthusiasm* emits an extremely high and expansive frequency and attracts to it the same in kind.

Highly sensitive artists emit *amplified* vibrations, whether they're aware of it or not. "Like seeks like"—in our world of frequencies, this is the basis of the Law of Attraction, which is why it's so important for us to have some command over our thoughts and feelings. Because when an artist falls into a hole and experiences the overwhelm of emotional upheaval, this torment, too, is amplified.

When we dramatize our negative feelings, all that energy unfolds into the next moment, and the moment after that, as a direct reflection of itself. This is how we perpetuate unhappiness. Likewise, we manifest what we fear most when we *think* about it too much. We are *not* our thinking, but—whether we're aware of it or not—we use our mind to manifest our lives.

Unless we learn to regulate our own frequency by making choices that uplift us, we will find ourselves at the mercy of our emotions. When we're at the mercy of our emotions, we fall easy prey to those who wish to instill fear, insecurity, and confusion as a means to manipulate and control—but that's another story.

Emotions play an important role in our lives, but because we have so little experience in how to *observe* them in real time, they tend to overwhelm us. Fear, anxiety, insecurity, grief, anger, and sadness overpower us. We feel like we have no control over these emotions, but we do.

As for lifting ourselves out of the humdrum habits of complaint, resentment, and crankiness, there's no easier way to shift your frequency than communing with nature. Ocean, mountain, forest, earth, sky, air, fire, animal, mineral, and plant—all are spirited entities. All have a life force. All offer expansive forms of communication. All are different vibrationally. And *all* will lift your attitude, mood, vibration, and spirit. In other words, we are surrounded by gifts from the planet that are designed to raise our *frequency*! We have only to *be* there, commune with them, and be grateful.

Techniques such as meditation, objective observation, falling in love with the mundane, and communing with nature are all tools for shifting our frequency. By using these techniques, we can raise our vibrational frequency at will. Out of this higher frequency, inspired answers, actions, and solutions are born.

Once these practices are a part of your life, no matter what's happening emotionally in your world, you'll be able to come to the present, observe what's occurring with you, allow it, acknowledge it, release it, and compose yourself in a breath or two. Okay, sometimes more—but you are operating in present time as opposed to becoming overwhelmed by a tsunami of emotions burying you in the past. You are practicing lifting your frequency at will.

It is in the stillness of the present moment that the voice of inspiration comes calling—as if a portal opens up at certain frequencies and more truth flows in.

I believe as more and more artists lift their frequencies at will, we create a path to *discover* what an enlightened existence might look like for all of humankind.

A Meditation Exercise: Expanding with Nature

Take thirty minutes *alone* in a natural setting of your choosing. It could be an unpopulated place in a park, on a beach, at a botanical garden, in a forest, by a river, or even in your own backyard. Try the following:

- Find a place that speaks to you, and take a seat.

- Turn off your phone.

- Look around, and breathe in the environment.

- Take in the size of the place.

- Observe.

- Listen.

- *See.*

- When thoughts arise, acknowledge them, and let them drift by like the clouds.

- Refocus your attention on something tiny: a blade of grass, an ant on its way home.

- Take in a rock. Can you see a single fleck of mica sparkling in the light?

- Find a flower. Observe the differences or similarities in the petals—note the pollen, stem, leaves, bees.

- Lie down and look up at the sky. Take in the size and shape of it.

- Note the movement of the clouds.

- Breathe in slowly and deeply—all the way down to your belly and beyond—as if your hips had lungs.

- Breathe in further, all the way to your toes.

- Exhale that which no longer serves you.

- Take about five or more deep breaths like this: include a beat of stillness when you are filled with air and a beat of stillness after you've exhaled.

- Sense the presence that you are. Observe from there.

- Feel yourself expanding as your senses open.

- When you are ready—and no sooner—end the exercise.

- Give thanks for the experience.

- On the walk back home, allow a stone to catch your eye. Ask the space it lives in if you might take it home. Pick it up and hold it to your heart. This is nature's acknowledgment. She is grateful that you *saw* her. You are practicing reverence.

- If you like, write about the experience in your journal when you return home.

When you breathe nature into your heart, you are connecting to spirit. It's that simple. Nature is spirit's most accessible expression.

Our planet is a living entity, alive and conscious. We are *of* her. She is the life force that supports all living things, and she *longs* to have a relationship with you. If you have not culti-vated a personal relationship with nature, you are missing out on your greatest teacher.

Still yourself

Breathe into your heart

Listen...

Nature is talking to you

When we take the time to breathe in nature—be it the ocean, mountains, forests, or sky—we immediately begin *expanding*. Because we are all connected, we stretch outward toward each other. Because we are spirit, we have no limits.

CHAPTER 7

You Are Not Your Story

"When I let go of what I am, I become what I might be."
—JOHN HEIDER

WE ALL HAVE OUR STORY. IT FOLLOWS US LIKE A SHADOW. OUR STORY IS a carefully crafted tale shaped by the trials and tribulations of our first twenty years or so: those trying, tender, terrible years we spend for the most part in school, where, in a hormonal frenzy, we try on identities like party clothes—longing to lure partnerships, admiration, and protectors—all the while bouncing off the walls of adolescence.

Our story always involves a list of circumstances and people that "done us wrong." It is our go-to justification when we fail to rise to the occasion. Our story is what we cling to when we stand panicked at the threshold of change.

But the most interesting thing about these foundational tales we cobble together is that we *repeat* our story throughout our lives in all kinds of imaginative but limiting ways—bending the truth to bolster evidence of its relevance.

If we are not actively leaning into our lives with a confident ability to make decisions about what we want and *choose* to do, we're probably busy spinning our story.

Here's an early version of mine: my mother left my father for my best friend's dad when I was eleven. The selfishness of that act, the lies, the betrayal, and the pain that followed for the two now-fractured families all cut deep. The event spun lifelong dramas for everyone involved—each with their own perspective on how they were victimized.

My father moved to Hollywood because that's where the work was, and hopefully, pain wasn't. My already-vague sense of him stretched across the continent until it became so thin, I could barely feel him at all.

My mother was not to be forgiven and certainly never to be trusted again. My answer was to silently put up with her. The subtext permeating my every behavior was, "You married the neighbor? You slept with my best friend's father and ended up in the same house that Dad found for you? Same bed! Seriously? You will never recover from the pain you've inflicted on others."

Awful of me, I know. Punishing. I sent her to Siberia. This part of my story repeated—she was the first, but not the last, person I banished to Siberia. Siberia is the ultimate "make-wrong," meaning, *I'm so right, and you're so wrong—you're dead to me.*

I felt emotionally banished as a child, and from that experience, I acquired the skills to banish others in the same way. I was especially good at it. There's a whole colony of friends who've disappointed me now living in Siberia.

There are even some who've reversed the game and sent *me* to Siberia. I have a number of people who've decided never to speak to me again. I'm not proud of it. You do what you can to make a relationship better, but at some point, you have to let go. Often, it's for the best.

Usually, our story repeats—variations on a theme, you might say, until we declare the game over! One of the many games the ego loves to play is "I'm righter, richer, thinner, smarter, prettier—as a matter of fact, I'm just plain *better* than you!" We've all played this game to some degree. We write it off as the American way.

It doesn't have to be—this crushing need to be better than someone else. But it takes practice not to engage in competition, gossip, and judgment—particularly when it's being directed *at* you. It takes practice to catch ourselves in *any* habitually unhealthy behavior. And it takes an act of will to make the decision to go another way. You have to be awake. You have to *want* change, particularly when the whole family is infected by this kind of dysfunction.

When my brother turned fifteen, my parents shipped him off to boarding school. And my best friend, now stepsister, hated the fact I lived with her father while she was forced to move to the city and take care of her shattered mother and two younger siblings. She was ten. It was brutal. Everyone pretended everything was okay. This is how my people cope.

Alone in my father's house with my mother and her new husband, I'd never felt so lonely. And to make matters worse, I could no longer hear my guides. It's not like they abandoned me; I just forgot to listen. I was distracted by all the anxiety, apprehension, and a sense of impending doom.

My body betrayed me as well, beginning its rocket-like journey from the sweetness of childhood to the utter confusion of adolescence. I was eleven when I got my first period, the same year of my mother's new marriage, which made me wildly vulnerable to the wall of emotions that came with it.

As my mother exchanged vows with her new husband, I remember bowing my head—not to pray, but to keep from passing out. The collective energy of the congregation overwhelmed me. It felt as if I couldn't separate my pain and confusion from everyone else's as we crowded into the tiny stone chapel—which also held 200 years of history and a vibe all its own.

Years later, I met a spiritual counselor who told me I was an empath—she said I absorbed everyone's feelings like a deluge without an umbrella. This information answered a few things for me. For instance, I have trouble in crowds. As a child, I would step into a packed elevator with my mother at, say, Lord & Taylor—wall-to-wall people, shoved into a tiny, moving room, energy ricocheting off the walls like ammo—it was too intense for me. I would pass out.

When department stores began installing escalators, I was convinced they did so because I'd passed out in their elevators and made a big fuss. I passed out at school assemblies. I passed out in the subway. I learned that anytime my entire circumference was *people*, it got dicey. My mother said I was claustrophobic and made me carry smelling salts, but I knew it had to do with receiving too much energy. I was short-circuiting.

Empathy Scale

If you've been told your entire life that you're "just too sensitive," chances are, you are. You are *too* sensitive for people on the lower spectrum of the empathy scale, and you will annoy them so much that they will let you know. Does any of this sound familiar?

Highly sensitive people:

- Are sensitive to light, sound, and smell.

- Are highly emotional.

- Are highly intuitive.

- Are often artists.

- Have a rich imagination and a powerful inner life.

- Love nature and quiet environments.

- Have a strong desire to help others.

Empaths take the experience of being highly sensitive a step further:

- They sense subtle energy, called shakti or prana, in Eastern traditions.

- They internalize the feelings of others energetically.

- They have trouble discerning someone else's energy from their own.

- They have a profound spiritual bond to nature and animals.

If you think about this distinction in terms of a sensitivity spectrum, empaths are on the far end, highly sensitive people are a little closer to the center, people with strong empathy are in the middle, and narcissists, sociopaths, and psychopaths are at the opposite end.

An empath grounded in love has a very strong healing frequency. They can lift the vibration of other people, populations, and the planet at large

Being highly sensitive or an empath is not better or worse—it just is, like your hair color. But it's good to know these high-sensitivity levels are not always understood or well tolerated by self or others.

Headed for Trouble

By the time I was twelve, I was armored up and headed for trouble. I didn't recognize myself through the anger and acting out that ensued. Add a healthy dose of hormones, and my emotions became so amplified, I lost myself completely.

It seemed I was ill-equipped for this world. I felt I had no value. I could find no recognition for who I was, much less the gifts I might have to offer. I had a vague sense of a power deep within, but with no one to *see* or acknowledge me, I assumed it was just some preteen fantasy.

I looked to teachers for some reflection of rightness in the world. Surely, it was a teacher's job to set an example of how this humanity thing was supposed to go. Surely, it was their responsibility to inspire and prepare us to face the challenges of this spirit-in-bodies experiment.

Instead, with the exception of one soulful English teacher and a dance mentor who I loved, school served up more unhappy people. Year after year, I felt my time usurped by teachers disconnected from their soul, failing to lead from the heart, fixated on ego, and often taking their frustrations out on their students.

I rebelled. I challenged them. I pointed out their injustices. I gave up. I'd leave campus. I walked away.

By the time I was thirteen, I was five-foot-six, fully developed, and doing my best to pass for twenty-one. I felt a power within, which I confused with my emerging sexuality. I was intoxicated by the sudden attention I was receiving for my pretty, young body and tested it out everywhere. Short skirt, cocked hip, yup—that got his attention. It seemed to me that this was the first thing I was any good at: catching the attention of horny young men.

The idea of having a boyfriend, someone to share all the confusion with, someone to have and to hold, felt like the answer to everything.

One afternoon hanging out at The Clock, an afterschool burger joint, I caught the attention of our very own, small-town, James Dean biker-type. *Wow!* I thought, *That's Perry Stevens! He's twenty-two, gorgeous, and has a motorcycle! And—oh, my God—he's looking right at me!*

It never occurred to me that there was a breed of twenty-year-old predators, well versed in girls too inexperienced and unempowered to say "no"—easy sexual prey to fuck and forget.

I burned my young leg on the exhaust pipe of his motorcycle and pretended it didn't hurt as he sped through the hills to his apartment in the attic of his parent's home. I didn't know what marijuana was but had already tried cigarettes with my brother—so no biggie. I pretended I was cool when, in fact, I was terrified. I pretended I had gotten high before, which was a lie. I pretended

I liked the sensation of the little control available to me sliding away in the smoke.

When he came at me like a linebacker, I resisted out of pure instinct. When he threatened to throw me out of his third-story window if I didn't have sex with him, I laughed, hoping it was a joke and knowing it wasn't.

When it was over, I thought he'd peed in me. I didn't know any better; I was thirteen. Then came the great pretend. I pretended to myself that I was okay. I pretended I was a "woman." And unbelievably, I pretended that I loved him and he loved me because the truth was just too awful.

Soon after, I was spotted leaving campus to meet my new "lover," who was visibly revving his motorcycle at the end of the long driveway outside my seventh-grade math class window. The school called my mother. It was a shitstorm, and I was sent to California to live with my father.

When Daydreams Return as Nightmares

The dreams of our childhood hold tremendous power. They often inform us of what we need most in life. From my lonely days of childhood, I dreamed of having a partner who loved me.

It started in the second grade. In order to survive the confinement, I taught myself to daydream. I'd look out the giant windows of the Buckingham Friends, Quaker school. Out across the enormous field of fresh-cut grass, past the eighteenth-century stone meeting house, and up into the hills—waiting for a prince on a white horse to arrive. He always did.

He would make his appearance through the trees, charge down the hill on his brilliant white steed, march into my second-grade class (on horseback), and announce, "Everything's okay—I'll just take Jocie. You all go about your business."

Off we'd go together, me on the back of his pure white pony to…I'm not sure where. The daydream ends with us charging up the hill. I indulged in this dream every day for a year.

It's not lost on me that I manifested an icky pedophile-biker version of my Prince Charming. Only instead of a white steed, he rode a Harley-Davidson up through the hills to his seedy attic apartment.

I had the power to manifest alright, but because I was so unhappy, I pulled in a low-vibration version of my dream.

We are manifesting moment to moment, whether we are aware of it or not. That's the nature of this game of life. Out of our deepest desires and needs, the dream will arrive in a form that reflects our thoughts and feelings at the time—in other words, our vibrational frequency.

You Are Not Your Story

The bottom line is: the stories we drag behind us to justify our unhappiness create bad habits. They transform us from *free*-spirited beings living in the *now* into fear-based beings living in the past. These are two very different vibrations, and the disparity between the frequencies of freedom and fear will attract two very different realities into our lives.

Because we craft our story from a litany of unfairness and traumas that have happened *to* us, we feel justified in feeling the victim.

Victims are defined by their *fear* of repeating traumas. That fear stunts our life choices, our self-esteem, and our sense of value.

When we live in fear, we draw to us the very thing we are most afraid of simply by the Law of Attraction. Our story then repeats itself in a variety of ways until we finally understand that it is completely irrelevant to the present moment, and we can, if we so *choose*, let it go.

Too often, we don't, because letting go of feelings can be terrifying! *Wait! I need this complication! This is ME! This lives at the core of who I am. I can't change who I am! Without this neurosis, I'm not ME!*

Nothing could be further from the truth.

The truth is: your *ego* is terrified YOU will show up and take back your life! Our personalities are desperately afraid of losing their hold over us. But we are so much more than our ego and personality.

In the end, we allow our stories to rule our behavior until we wake up to the fact that we *use* our stories to make excuses for the limitations we place on ourselves.

We are neither our fears nor our feelings, and the *stories* we drag behind us keep us tethered to the past. They're just memories— strong, emotional, and intriguing, yes, but about as important as dust.

We are new to the planet. I believe humanity is in the process of growing up. Instead of *thinking* of our lives as a series of personal dramas and indulging in them as we would a daily soap opera, we are waking up to what we're capable of when we dream of what is best for the whole human condition.

We do well when we focus on becoming the best human we can be and seek our own unique way to contribute to society. Then, the path becomes clearer, and we're less likely to get lost in all the dramas that spin around us.

You are not defined by your personal history

You are not defined by your thoughts or emotions

The idea is not to change *who you are*

The idea is to become *who you are*

The energy that is YOU

Is only experienced in the moment

Like a breath of air

Like a heartbeat

YOU

The Structure of a Dream

Whereas an actor is stuck with the parameters of the story he's given, *you* are not. You can change from a life that is happening *to* you to a life *you* create moment to moment:

- Where you live

- What you do for a living

- Partnership and marriage

- Relationship with friends and family

- How you eat

- How you spend your time

- Your healthy routines vs. your unhealthy routines

- Your spiritual beliefs

- Your habits and practices

These structural choices apply to every life, and every one of these choices is under your command.

Here are some questions actors consider when tasked with creating the life of another. All can be applied to consciously creating a life of your own making.

Actor Creating A Character	Person Creating A Life	
Where am I?	Where do I want to be?	
What do I want in this scene?	What do I want for my life?	
What am I doing about it?	What am I doing about it?	
What will happen if I don't get it?	How will I feel if I fail to go after it?	
What's happening on the surface?	What does my life look like to others?	

Actor Creating A Character	Person Creating A Life
What's going on underneath?	What is happening on a deeper, more intimate level?
Does my character want to change?	What do I want to change?
What am I afraid of?	What fears do I want to let go of?
How does that fear affect me?	What can I do about that fear?
Who supports me in the story?	Who uplifts me?
Who wishes me ill, and why?	Who brings me down, and why?
What are my obstacles?	What do I need to overcome?
What am I doing about it?	What am I doing about it?
What else can I do about it?	What else can I do about it?
Who do I love and why?	Who do I love and why?
How do I love?	How do I show my love? How can I show my love?
How do I treat myself?	How can I be kinder to myself and others?
What am I hiding?	What am I hiding from others and myself?
How do my secrets affect me?	How do my secrets affect me, and what can I do about it?

Knowing what you want is the beginning. *Being* what you want by *doing* the things you'd do if you already had it will raise your frequency and attract *it* to you.

We intuitively *want* to make the kind of changes that lead us to our best selves, but without knowing how, we sometimes look for people to *tell* us the answers. We give away our power and open ourselves to manipulation when we follow someone else's prescription for enlightenment. Cults take advantage of seekers by dangling bits of truth as bait. Before you know it, they are taking your money and "graduating" you up some ladder of trade-marked "truth" with control mechanisms. When you spot a rich guy sitting atop a pyramid of admirers, pretending benevolence while claiming to have all the answers, run!

Only *you* know what's best for you. No one else has *your* answers. If you accept this and turn toward yourself, I promise you will find what you're looking for. And when you do, keep it private. As I tell my students, "Be it—don't *tell* it."

Taking responsibility for the construction of your life and how you spend your time is essential to creating a life with purpose. Anyone who chooses can change their story. Life is a blank canvas. Go ahead: write a great story for yourself! Better yet, let your heart dictate it!

Imagine

How do you make your dreams come true?

Imagining is step one. When you imagine what you want, you must *see* yourself in the role.

When I ask actors about their dream, they often tell me, "I want to work in the best films, with the best scripts, with the best directors."

The problem is they're *fantasizing*. They're thinking about artists who have those things already and wishing they were those people. The problem is: it's not *their* dream, so *they* are not in the picture! It's as if they are superimposing their face on somebody else's hard work.

If you can't *see* yourself—in a very specific way—as you develop the dream from your own unique perspective, then no one else will be able to either.

Madonna didn't fashion her career after another artist. She didn't operate on "I want to be the best" and then move forward, hoping it would somehow happen. No, she envisioned and *projected* an inspired idea of herself and her music—and then went about taking the tens of thousands of *steps* she needed to fulfill that vision.

The same goes for Charlie Chaplin, Marilyn Monroe, Cher, Cary Grant, Katharine Hepburn, Joni Mitchell, Jerry Lewis, and so many more. The greatest actors and musicians of all time are successful because they project *themselves* into the part. They *embrace* their particular uniqueness and go to work. They honor themselves by believing they have something exceptional to offer, something unlike anyone else. They do. We all do!

Many artists are insecure. Their low self-esteem gets in the way of believing in themselves. They're afraid of failing. They're afraid of being hurt. Because of this fear, they lock their dreams away and *fantasize* instead. Fantasizing isn't necessarily a bad thing, but it won't inspire you to take the actions you need because you don't really believe the fantasy is real.

The difference between a fantasy and a dream or vision for yourself is:

- A FANTASY is safe because it involves the impossible or the improbable. It doesn't disturb or insist. It is designed to pacify, like a lollipop.

- A DREAM is *unsafe* because it involves the heart. It is a cherished aspiration, ambition, or ideal, and as such—it *demands* action. The heart knows that realizing a dream risks failure. If the person is too afraid of failing, they will bury their dream. Sometimes they keep it a secret even from themselves.

Failing, learning from failing, and getting back up—over and over again—is as important to getting what you want as learning how to walk. You need to believe in your dream enough to withstand the slings and arrows that are built into all growth.

I've been known to tell actors, "If you can see it, you can have it." Imagining is the most powerful form of thought. Imagine *yourself* in the dream. Honor and apply the very things that make you the unique individual you are.

The Dream

If you could have anything you want, barring all obstacles, what would it be?

Still yourself, ask the question, trust, and *listen* to what your heart has to say about why you are here in this life. It may not come right away; just keep asking. When the heart speaks, you will *see* yourself in the dream. You'll not only *know* it's possible—you'll *feel* like it's your destiny.

When YOU are projected into your *vision*, not only do you *see* yourself doing the things necessary to attain it, you also have the necessary enthusiasm to follow through. That's when the work becomes fun! That's when you become *eager* to work harder than you've ever imagined. That's when you begin working for *yourself* and living your own life. That's when you *believe*.

Know this: you will face challenges. You will get hurt. You'll have good days and bad days. You will sometimes experience confusion and even doubt. That's called living. So, as long as all those things are on the menu anyway, you might as well go after your heart's desire. Once you have your finger on the pulse of your dream, it will easily dictate the *goals* you'll need to meet to realize it.

Set Goals

Your goals are the targets you'll need to set that add up to the dream. They're about *organizing* the work so that it can be executed. For instance, if your dream is to publish a book, an early goal will be a first draft.

But a first draft is only one of many goals you'll need to meet. Outlines, chapters, rewrites, publishing, and promotion are some of the others. To publish a book, you'll need to accomplish many, many goals (both creative and administrative) by taking the thousands of *steps* necessary to meet them. When you've taken all the steps and met all the goals, you will have manifested the dream.

For example, a small but foundational goal of any actor is joining The Screen Actors Guild. I ask beginning actors to make a list of all the *steps* they could take to accomplish that goal. They, of course, want me to tell them what those steps are—and then how to accomplish them. But it is *discovering* the steps for yourself and taking them that earns you the confidence to move on to *larger* goals.

The dream determines the goals. The goals determine the steps.

Take the Steps

To achieve your *goals*, you'll need to take the many, many steps that make up your journey. The steps are the daily *actions* you take to achieve your goals. Every time you *do* something, you take another *step*. Without accomplishing the necessary steps, it's all in your head.

Step-by-step programs are the organized lists of things you need to do to achieve your goals: "In order to have this, I have to *do* that."

By creating these lists, the path appears—a road map you can follow and believe in. It is taking the *steps* necessary to complete your *goals* that add up to *manifesting* your dream.

Sorry, no shortcuts. That's a fantasy.

Goal-Setting Example

Structure	Dream	Goals	Step-By-Step Program
WHERE TO LIVE? Say you rent a one-bedroom apartment in Los Angeles.	Your dream is to rent a one-bedroom apartment on the Upper West side of Manhattan.	You will certainly need to create a budget to move. **1. CREATE A BUDGET**	Here is a starter list of obvious steps: *Research the cost of one-bedroom apartments in the area you want *Research the cost of physically moving there *Research the kind of work you could get in New York to support your new life
		Let's say you're falling short on the money needed to cover your budget. Your next goal might be: **2. MAKE MORE MONEY** Remember, it's not about how long it takes; it's about being your dream by doing the things you'd do if you already had it. Your dream won't magically appear in the future—unless you live it by doing it NOW.	**List the steps you can take to make the money you need to move:** *Work more hours *Sell my car *Have a garage sale *List "100 ways I could make money" (a very powerful exercise) **As you're working on steps, you will inevitably come up with more steps that turn into GOALS. For example, one of your steps under "making more money" might be:** *Get a second, third, or better job Or even: *Obtain new credentials, like a degree **STEPS that become GOALS are solutions that call for their own series of steps.**

Once you put your destination on the map, it's easy to plot a course to get there. One action daily will take you one step closer to your ideal. More steps daily will get you there even faster.

Exercise: To-Do List

When advising actors on their careers, I tell them to write up their goals in great detail. The more specific their desires, the more they will reveal the concrete steps they need to take to meet their goals and manifest their dreams. Here's an exercise you can apply to your day-to-day goals.

Close your eyes and breathe into your heart.

Inhale: I breathe in energy.

Exhale: I breathe out exhaustion.

Continue for ten minutes. Then, open your journal:

- Write three simple goals you can accomplish today. For example:

  * I want to clean and reorganize the guest-room closet.

  * I want to write the first draft of a logline for my new script.

  * I want to cook a good vegetarian meal for dinner tonight.

- Next, create a simple plan to accomplish each.

  * 9:00 to 10:30 a.m.—Go to the open-air market and get fresh vegetables for a pasta dish tonight.

  * 10:30 to 11:30 a.m.—Empty the entire closet into three areas: keep, throw away, and give away.

  * 11:30 to 12:30 p.m.—Clean the interior of the closet. Toss the "throw away" stuff in the trash. Box up the "give away" stuff and put it in the trunk of the car to donate.

  * 12:30 to 1:00 p.m.—Eat lunch.

  * 1:30 to 2:00 p.m.—Walk.

  * 2:00 to 2:30 p.m.—Reorganize the things we're keeping in the new closet space.

  * 2:45 to 3:00 p.m.—Meditate.

  * 3:00 to 4:00 p.m.—Research the greatest loglines in history.

  * 4:00 to 4:30 p.m.—Write the first draft of my logline.

  * 4:30 to 5:30 p.m.—Walk/exercise.

  * 5:30 to 6:00 p.m.—Prep veggies for pasta dish.

- Execute your plan.

- Return to this place in your journal at the end of the day and check off what you accomplished.

This is an easy exercise in manifestation.

BIG dreams require that you believe in them with all your heart. When you can project your utterly unique qualities into your dream, the organization and execution of that dream won't feel like work. It will feel like you are living the life *you* choose.

CHAPTER 8

Find *You*—Let the Rest Go

"Is it so bad, then, to be misunderstood? Pythagoras was misunderstood, and Socrates, and Jesus, and Luther, and Copernicus, and Galileo, and Newton, and every pure and wise spirit that ever took flesh. To be great is to be misunderstood."

—RALPH WALDO EMERSON

BACK WHEN I WAS THIRTEEN YEARS OLD AND THROWN OUT OF MY FIRST school for fleeing campus on the back of Perry Stevens's motorcycle, my mother and stepfather were at a loss as to what to do with me. They settled on banishing me to California to live with my father. Some banishment. I had to go live at the beach with my dad, who may have been absent in my early childhood but really showed up for me as a troubled teen.

Trying his hand at single parenting—while at the same time having no idea how long I'd be with him—my father rented a two-bedroom cottage on Topanga Beach in Malibu, California. The rooms were teeny-tiny, but the place was perfect in every way. It had a large cedar deck smack on the sand and a wood-burning fireplace for cold nights. What more could you want?

There was even a set of stairs on the side of the house that led up to a private room with a bed, a toilet, a sink, an illegally plumbed shower, and astonishing views of the sea. I wasn't allowed to go in that room because it was saved for my brother, who was serving in Vietnam.

With that one gesture—a house on the beach, with a room for my brother, who I might or might not ever see again—I suddenly saw my father as a hero. He had rented a home he felt his children would love. Other than in the movies, I'd never seen a grown-up put their child's needs before their own. It was the first time since Gracie that I remember feeling loved.

There were fifteen to twenty houses strung together on West Topanga Beach Road, some of them little more than shacks—all of them now long gone. Topanga was built on a ninety-nine-year land lease, and those ninety-nine years ran out. There was the usual outcry of displacement, and many tears were shed as the bulldozers erased not only a soulful beach community but a way of life, leaving nothing behind but a sterile state beach and a lot of broken hearts. But that was many years ago.

Back when my father rented the little house with the blue ceramic fish that served as a door latch on the outside gate—back then, Topanga Beach was magic. The houses were linked together on the roadside by a patchwork of handmade fences—barriers forming a defense against any trespassers who might wander down the narrow road looking for beach access.

Conversely, on the beach side, everything was wide open. Houses, sand, sun, and sea—one rambling property bled seamlessly into the next. Every house had kids, dogs roamed free, no one locked their doors, and everyone knew your name.

Topanga was a surfer's paradise, where the waves crashed endlessly and echoed back from the opposite hillside. Pretty enchanting stuff.

I arrived in California at the end of seventh grade and spent a long, hot summer on the beach before I was sent to boarding school. I would wake up in the morning, throw on a bathing suit, and not take it off until I hit the sheets at night—that is, until my father ruled that when the sun went down, you had to dress in *real* clothes.

The ocean was the star at Topanga. No matter how early I stepped out on the deck, there were surfers in the water reveling in their morning meditation. Long boards between their legs, they sat in the water, waiting for the waves to roll right.

Even when the sea sat glassy and the absence of wind felt like God was holding his breath, beautiful men from age five to fifty—and even a few girls—sat in the water patiently waiting for the dragon to wake up and play with them again.

Much of the time, the energy that blew in with the waves was so spirited it overwhelmed me. Like walking in a thunderstorm, the negative ions stirred my brain in a wild sort of way and reminded me that I was indeed a part of a giant miracle. The ocean is BIG nature, and even though I couldn't *hear* her in the same way that I could my trees, the power of the sea restored the magic in me.

My father decided it was better to have kids at our house than for me to go getting into trouble elsewhere, so our kitchen was the place to go for an endless stream of Tab, Fresca, and ham and cheese sandwiches on rye—the best! This made my dad pretty popular with my new beach friends, plus he was an actor, and everybody loves an actor.

One night at a party on the beach—on an evening lit by the moon, with kids making out to "Be My Baby" by The Ronettes—a girl I didn't know came to me in a frantic state. "I've lost my necklace," she said. "Please, I know you can find it."

I tried to dissuade her, but Cathy, as she was called, pleaded with me. "It was my grandmother's, and she's telling me you can find it!"

Maybe because I was touched by her grandmother's faith in me, maybe because I'd indulged in a fair amount of beer, or maybe because the god of lost objects has always been a friend to me, I started looking.

Relying on instinct alone, I began scanning the beach like a human Geiger counter in an effort to narrow down the area of possibility. The party was pretty sprawled out, but in a matter of ten minutes or so, I managed to zero in on a small section of sand and rocks near a gnarly driftwood log. It felt "hot" to me. Cathy was ecstatic. "Yes, yes, I was here!" she chirped, encouraging me in my search.

I asked her to sit on the log and be still as I ran my hands over the sand, seeking a connection. Some little kids arrived with a flashlight, and then others, heightening the pressure for success.

Hands over sand, the heat of intuition, dig, sift, repeat.

I don't know why I had such certainty. Part of it was the wonder of youth when all possibility is stretched out before you, and part of it was that I could *see* myself finding the thing—but on the fourth or fifth try, my hands slid through the sand, and there, hanging from my fingers, was Cathy's necklace.

My guides were back!

The magic of the sea, the beauty of that community, and my father's acts of love restored my faith in life. I discovered that nature, beauty, and love were my measures for a life well-lived. They still hold as the basic foundations of my life.

Called Upon

It was the most important question my father ever asked me: "Jocie, if you could have anything in the world, barring all obstacles, what would you want?"

I have asked myself that question at various junctures in my life. It has proven to be a profound tool for transformation.

When I came to California to live with him, he asked me that question for the first time. My answer was immediate: "I want to live with you at the beach and go to public school."

That was impossible, whether because my dad spent so much time on location or because raising a precocious thirteen-year-old girl alone seemed too terrifying. Either way, after a glorious summer on Topanga Beach, I was sent away to a boarding school in Ojai, California, about two hours north of Malibu.

Happy Valley, as it was called, was founded in 1946 by Aldous Huxley, J. Krishnamurti, and Rosalind Rajagopal, among others. I'm pretty sure it was *not* the school these great minds had envisioned by the time I got there, but they clearly chose Ojai because it's one of those rare power spots. The Ojai Valley is surrounded by a ring of mountains. Once you're surrounded by a circle of mountains like that, it's possible to get caught up in the crossfire of energy that whips across the valley floor, bouncing from one mountain to another. They talk to each other, those mountain entities—there's a BIG energy force there!

My father drove up every Sunday to bring me a care package and take me out to lunch at a fancy hotel nearby. He was the only parent who visited every Sunday, so I began taking a different girl to lunch every week to give them something to look forward to as well.

One night in the dormitory, two girls came to my room totally freaked out. Michelle had started to pierce Penny's ears, but halfway through the deal, they both panicked. As I was the only one in the dorm who *had* pierced ears, I was the obvious "go-to" girl for expertise. Both friends were crying, and Penny had blood dripping from her right lobe.

There was nothing to do but take charge. I ordered Michelle to get a bowl of ice and began sterilizing a needle with a Diamond strike-anywhere match. Knowing they would come in handy for smoking and other illicit things, I'd pilfered a box from the beach house along with a few other hard-for-a-thirteen-year-old-girl-to-obtain goodies, like cigarettes and Valium.

My father, Henry, had *everything* in our little beach house—from a present-wrapping department to a large box of backup essentials like aspirin, shampoo, bug spray, tampons, Parliaments, Dial soap (the smell of which still sends me into sense-memory heaven), and many boxes of Diamond strike-anywhere matches. I liked to impress my friends by striking them on the zipper of my jeans or from behind my front teeth. I think I started smoking cigarettes just to strike the coolest matches in the world in odd places.

The earrings Penny had chosen were a pale turquoise—small oval stones that matched her kind, young eyes. I dropped them into a dish of alcohol. Less than fifteen minutes later, the deal was done. I had to move quickly and baby-talk her through the whole thing, or I might have passed out myself.

I learned that when in doubt, it's best to assume the position of utter confidence. This became a reliable cover for insecurity, one I used often.

I pierced a dozen pairs of ears before I got thrown out of Happy Valley for—wait for it...*Not* for piercing ears. Not for baking Benzedrine into brownies and feeding them to the dorm mother, who had to be carted off to the hospital for heart palpitations. Not for coming on to the married twenty-nine-year-old art teacher. Not even for planting marijuana seeds by the stream, which turned out to be the perfect environment for weed to grow wild. Nope! I finally got thrown out for leaving campus in the dead of night to meet a twenty-seven-year-old townie on a motorcycle—this one had spent some time in jail.

It was the second school I'd been thrown out of for that kind of behavior. The second motorcycle incident as well. But it worked! I got sent back to my dad.

Degraded and ashamed, I pretended I didn't care about anything, but the fact was I'd gotten my wish. I'd gotten the thing I wanted more than anything in the world: to live at the beach with my dad and go to public school.

And I had learned two important lessons:

1. I'd learned from my father—who must have been terrified at the prospect of parenting an out-of-control thirteen-year-old—that when circumstances present themselves, you rise to the occasion. I'd been called upon in a crisis, and I'd stepped up. I'd taken charge of the bloody earlobes!

2. I'd discovered I could get what I wanted. The question became: how do you get what you want without destroying your self-esteem and shaming yourself in the process?

You Are Not Your Emotions

Let's face it: it's hard to let go of shame. We also have trouble letting go of regret, anger, jealousy, bitterness, anxiety, and blame. It hurts us to let go of lovers, friends, jobs, arguments, and being right, even when we know we're wrong. We have habits we *know* we'd be better off without. When we recognize this and summon the courage to let go, we're rewarded with new space and a more honest version of ourselves.

Buried grief may be the hardest of all to let go of, but with a little practice, we can reconcile even the most difficult emotions by accepting them as messages from our subconscious. These messages tell us we are ready to release an injured self from the past. A piece of us we left behind. A part of us that holds us back because it's holding on—to be heard, understood, experienced, loved, and released.

When the damaged self receives the space to safely express what happened, *and* we meet the ensuing emotions with compassion and understanding, the trapped feelings release—and the traumatized self can integrate. In other words, a healing takes place. Shamans call this *soul retrieval*. As a process, it takes unconditional love from someone who knows how to listen.

Sometimes, a student will fall into grief in a critique because they feel vulnerable, and vulnerability can trigger past traumas. When that happens, I don't get into *why* they're overwhelmed. That's for another time and place. But when they're holding back a wall of tears, there's little chance of them returning to the present unless they regain some control.

So, I tell them, "Go ahead...let it go. Cry. Cry hard. Cry deep. Cry so hard and so deep you move through it quickly—and *on purpose*."

When we hold back tears, we get stuck. It feels counterintuitive, I know, but when grief overwhelms us, we *can* let go of our resistance to the tears and instead *choose* to move through. We can go *with* the momentum instead of against it. I'll say, "Cry harder. Fake it a little. Acting badly in this situation is a great move. It might even make us laugh!"

The idea is to take hold of the reins and steer the runaway emotion in the direction of our choice. I'm not invalidating the trauma, as there's definitely something there—but by letting go of resistance and telling ourselves to cry harder, we release the tears *on purpose*. We take control.

This act alone won't integrate the grief. To do that, you have to give the memory a compassionate space to express itself and feel understood. But by asking an actor to "cry harder," I hope to teach them how to let go of resistance and intentionally *push on* their emotions, thereby granting the *being* the control to move forward.

Once they gain even the slightest control, they can begin to make choices again. For instance, they can choose to observe their feelings: *Wow, that's a lot of emotion. I wonder what all this is about? Oh, God, I think I have some snot running down my lip.*

More than one actor has found themselves in a puddle of tears, only to run to the mirror to observe what it looked like! The *person* is crying. The *artist* wants to see what that's all about!

Or, you can take note of what triggered you and take it up at a later date. *This is not the time and place for what I'm feeling. I'm going to note this, let it go for now, and take it back up at a time of my choosing.*

All three choices—push harder, observe, take note for later—put *you* in charge of your emotions.

Emotions are a grand invention. Their sneaky collaboration with the nervous system to gang up and overwhelm us like the boogie man is very effective. But no matter how much they try to scare us, we're bigger than they are. We are senior. Our emotions are just equipment in need of an upgrade. They were designed for consciousness to *experience*—but like *thinking*, we're so enamored with their brilliance that we assume them as our identity.

How many times have you heard "You can't control how you feel"? Well, okay, we all have trapped feelings that sneak up on us and demand to be heard. But with awareness, we can learn to determine the time and place for our expressions. With practice, we can choose when and how we release them. We are neither our thinking nor our emotions. We are bigger—much, much bigger.

When I observe my emotions without judgment, I see that in their most primitive form, emotions serve to protect us. They're anchored in fear. *Don't go down that road again. Remember—you almost died!* Fear is very successful at keeping us alive, but in our evolutionary leap toward a *realized* humanity, fear becomes a real problem. It attaches itself to everything, and like gum on the bottom of your shoe, it's going to stick around—unless you recognize it's there and find a way to *let it go*.

Meditation and observation are the antidotes to fear. Once we find that place of stillness, even for a second, past and future slip aside— and in that gap, we create a space for the presence of truth to arrive.

Even a tiny sliver of awareness goes a long, long way. Being awake in the moment grants us the ability to maintain mental calmness and composure under difficult circumstances—and in so doing, we enjoy the sweetness of equanimity.

Drop the Bone

One of the most inspiring things actors do is remind us we have command over our emotions. They are living examples of our ability to conjure emotion at will. Not only do they summon the entire spectrum of feelings and sensations, they must let go of their fear of performing to do so. Actors need to be reminded that they can apply to their lives what they do in their work.

The problem is we love emotions! Sometimes we even feed on them. Emotions amplify experience, and that's why we're here. This three-dimensional life on Earth in time and space is all about experience. Emotional experiences make us feel real, solid, alive!

At our studio, we ask artists to leave their personal problems outside the theatre door as a way of practicing professional etiquette. When an actor in class starts spewing their personal drama during a critique, I am unsympathetic.

"Drop the bone," I'm known to say.

They look at me, confused and defensive. Usually, they're fighting to be right. They are outraged at something they see as a massive injustice. Letting go of their "rightness" feels like it might just kill them. There's no objectivity, no looking at the problem from a different point of view. They are hunkered down, needing to be right, and the last thing they want to do is let go!

"Does your jaw hurt?" I ask.

"What?" they answer, confused, gawking at me, defensive.

"It's okay," I say, wanting to gentle them. It's not like I haven't experienced these feelings myself. "Don't worry, just...drop the bone."

"What?!" They sense where the conversation is going.

"Just pry open your teeth and let it go," I say with as much compassion as I can muster for someone looking like they might just kill me. Usually, we end up laughing.

Letting Go

Whenever you feel dug in, stuck, or chomping down on the bone of righteousness, know that you are coming up short of your full potential. Letting go, even for a few seconds, will leave space for something *new* to arrive—a wise practice in both life and art.

Without awareness of the energetic being inside all this marvelous apparatus, we move through life like the top hat, thimble, or boot on a Monopoly board. Around and around the playing field we go, trying to acquire money and power and *things*. We don't realize we have shrunk ourselves down to a weensy representation of something HUGE and glorious.

Suddenly, we're not spirit at all—we're Janet, who is married to Wilson and has two children and a split-level house in the Poconos. We are a Democrat or a Republican. We are black, white, brown, or yellow. We believe in somebody else's description of

God. We believe in money, or communism, or witchcraft. We are good, or we are bad. *They* are good, or they are bad. We identify with our thoughts, our emotions, our things, and everything we see on screens. We go through life creating problems, so we can *identify* with the problems and *experience* the emotions they kick up. Solve it or not, we love a juicy problem. Like a dog with a bone, we like to gnaw on it for as long as possible and growl at anyone who threatens to take it away.

Who wants to be an invisible spirit anyway? We want to be *pretty*. We want to feel admired. We want to *be* these amazing bodies we occupy. We want to *be* our fabulous minds. We don't want to be *in* the moment; we want to THINK about things in a way that will conjure problems and the emotions that come with them. Whether or not we solve those problems, we're damn sure life would be impossibly boring without them.

We're like a genie in a bottle who would rather *be* the bottle!

Still, letting go is easy. It's a consideration. A decision to *release* our love for complication and embrace a simple concept: we are pure energetic beings inside bodies, and once we get to know the *being* beyond our personality, we are capable of anything.

As we practice letting go of the past and moving into the NOW, we become part of the great awakening of our time. We are evolving. We are ascending. We are taking a giant leap with a tiny step.

Past and future are tenses of the mind. We *think* about the past, we *think* about the future, and we use our precious present to do so. To *be* in the NOW, we have to let go of all that *thinking*. At least some of the time.

Exercise: Letting Go

Here is an exercise to help you.

Close your eyes and listen to your breath for ten minutes.

Inhale: I breathe in light.

Exhale: I exhale darkness.

Repeat for ten minutes. As you meditate:

- Focus your attention on the black space behind your eyes—this is your mental screen. See yourself watching this screen as if you were watching a movie.

- When thoughts arrive, project them onto this screen. Allowing them in doesn't mean you want them—it means you *allow* them to be, just as you *allow* them to pass.

- Realize you are observing your thoughts as you would watch a movie or TV. *You* are not your thoughts, just as *you* are not the movie that captures your attention.

- Allow them to be, and simply let them go. Let them drift by slowly and fade away.

- You are entering the present moment of NOW.

- After ten minutes (or longer if you like), open your eyes. Breathe into your heart.

Complete the following exercise in your journal if you wish:

- List three things you'd like to let go of—maybe smoking, gossiping, or procrastinating (not doing the very things you know will make you happy).

- Choose one you really cling to.

- Now, write a letter in your journal thanking *this item* for how it has served you. *Here is how I identified with you. Here is what you gave me. Thank you for these things.*

- Announce that you are giving it up, close your eyes, say goodbye, and let it go.

- Open your eyes.

- Is it still there?

How do we let go of this stuff and create more space in our lives? Well, we *let it go.*

Sorry, that's it. You make a decision—and let it go. When it comes up again (and it will), say to yourself, "Oh yeah, I let that go." That's it—nothing more! Anything more is a self-imposed complication.

When it comes up again, clean the kitchen, drink a glass of water, read a book, take a walk—do *anything* else. After practicing this a while, your awareness will begin to erode the attachment. You'll spot the habit more easily. Whether it be judging, complaining, or a physical habit like eating too much sugar—you'll become aware that you are doing it (or *about* to) and let it go. You'll be able to stop, look at it, and choose to move on in a different way.

Don't analyze, battle, or reconsider—those are sure ways to lose. Don't ponder. Simply *do* the practice.

Learning this is an enormous confidence booster! It is a huge step in trusting yourself to do the right thing for YOU.

If you fail, fine. It happens. Start over.

CHAPTER 9

Write Your Own Story

"Be yourself; no base imitator of another, but your best self. There is something which you can do better than another. Listen to the inward voice and bravely obey that. Do the things at which you are great, not what you were never made for."

—RALPH WALDO EMERSON, SELF-RELIANCE

AFTER GETTING THROWN OUT OF HAPPY VALLEY, I LIVED AT THE BEACH with my dad and went to public school for a year or so. I spent roughly six months in junior high, and after another glorious summer on Topanga Beach, I started freshman year at the local high school. It was fun taking the bus to school with my beach buddies, but—although I loved living with my dad as well as the change in culture—something in me said it was time to go home. I didn't know why, but I felt like a fish out of water.

I didn't wait until the end of the school year. I returned home to Snedens and went to a few more schools on the East Coast. Somehow, I was always the "new girl"—always arriving in the middle of the year under mysterious circumstances. Everyone knew who I was. I knew no one. Rumors thrived.

I learned to stand tall and hang my limbs to feign a cool, deep relaxation that didn't exist. I looked unruffled on the outside—inside, I felt like I was entering a war zone.

I became pretty good at pretending. The only sign of the real me—whom I hadn't seen since I last talked to trees—was an uncanny ability to tell people what they *knew* in their bones but didn't yet *see* about themselves. I'd just pick things up out of the space around them.

I loved to talk—no matter the subject, no need for experience. I would *act* with such a show of confidence, I'd fool myself. It was a cover for insecurity, of course. I took on the opposite of anxiety. I feigned a cool, apathetic demeanor and wore it like armor. I was arrogant, self-centered, and off-putting—I had no idea how others were responding to me, nor did I care. I am still chasing back bad habits born of a lifetime of protecting my insecurities. Life is a practice.

My father liked to tell a story about how he took me to a birthday party for Sally Field, and I sat down with the head of a major motion picture studio and entertained him with tales of how he should run his business—for an hour. I was fourteen at the time. I remember the party, not the incident, but it sounds like me. I was a talker.

The last school I attended was the Professional Children's School. PCS was a specialized school in Midtown Manhattan for child actors, musicians, and dancers—and, sometimes, the *children* of such artists. I was sixteen and living with my mother and stepfather when I heard about the school from an older girl I admired. She talked about how the kids from the Broadway musical *Oliver!* went there, and how casting directors regularly cast kids from the school for all kinds of projects. Best of all, the hours were only from 10 to 2! I thought surely I could hack four hours of school a day.

I begged my parents to let me go. It was so unusual for me to show any interest in school that my mother and father—who rarely spoke to each other—agreed to let me take the hour-plus commute from Snedens to the city. I'd walk to the bus stop on route 9W, which dropped me off on the city side of the George Washington Bridge at 178th street. From there, I took the A train down to 59th at Columbus Circle. The school was only a few blocks from there. What an adventure! I was sixteen years old, and New York was at my fingertips.

After school, we took classes in dance, acting, and/or music. There was a flurry of ballerinas destined for fine companies. I loved taking class with them at the Carnegie Hall studios. I thought I'd become a dancer for a while, but I sensed I wasn't tough enough to cut it.

I was also cast in a few dance projects for trade shows and several teen runway events. Although I'd been involved in school plays and dance programs at every school I'd attended, being hired professionally was fun! The money wasn't much, but it opened my eyes to a whole new world. I suddenly dreamed of living on my own in the city and paying my way as a performer of some kind.

Toward the end of the eleventh grade, my father, who was working in New York, got a call from the headmistress of the school to come in for a chat.

Years later, he told me the story of how Mrs. Mundy, an attractive woman with a French air about her, rushed in, apologized for being late, opened her office door, and ushered him in. Clickety-clacking across the wooden floor in her nonsensible heels, she plopped down at her desk and slipped off her shoes to free her aching feet.

My father found something sexy in her arrival and considered asking her out, but thought better of it as she offered him the chair opposite her. As he took a seat—literally hat in hand—he felt a sense of impending doom. With a sober look, the headmistress finally spoke. "You know, Henry, school is not for everyone."

The sentence hung in the air a while. My father did his best to contain his mounting alarm. "What are you telling me?" he answered.

"Well…" Mrs. Mundy searched for the words.

"Are you telling me I should let my daughter *DROP OUT OF HIGH SCHOOL*?!"

The headmistress took a deep breath and hit him with the facts: "Well, Jocelyn has attended maybe a third of her classes so far this year. She doesn't have enough credits to go into her senior year. Do you think she'll be up for repeating the eleventh grade?"

My father was appalled. He dropped his head in his hands in despair. He had been educated by Jesuits. He'd debated *in Latin* at Saint Joseph's University in Philadelphia. He believed in the power of education, and my failure to thrive in school became his failure as a father.

"She's pretty smart, Henry. I think she'll be okay," said the woman bearing bad news.

Emancipation

My father summoned me to the Russian Tea Room for lunch the next day. I had the chicken Kiev, and when the waiter made that first theatrical cut, and the butter squirted out on cue, I felt the blood leave my heart as I saw the disappointment in my father's eyes.

He took a deep breath and sighed dramatically. "Jocie, if you could have anything in the world, barring all obstacles, what would you want?"

I love this question. "I want to drop out of school and begin my life," I answered with 100 percent certainty.

Another sigh. My father was a world-class sigher. He tried again. "Okay. But *then* what would you want? What do you want to *be*?"

"Free," I said, as if I were entitled.

"FREE TO DO WHAT?!" he bellowed. All the waiters in the room looked at the floor.

My father would win any oratory dispute, hands down. He was an actor, after all, an actor who had debated in Latin at Saint Joseph's University—for some reason, I found this particularly impressive. I still do.

"I don't know!" I shot back. "I need to go looking for it. But when I find it, I'll know! Trust me: I'll know."

An uncomfortable silence set in. I pushed a small piece of chicken around the circumference of my plate until I gained the courage to look up again. Finally, I snuck a peek. We locked eyes, staring at each other until something melted.

"Well…if you can get a job, I guess you can quit school," my father said to me, sadder and madder than I've ever seen him.

I had a job in twenty-four hours. I was free! My life could finally begin!

I left my mother's home, moved into the city, crashed with friends, and waitressed at multiple 2nd Avenue pubs. I was seventeen. The legal age to serve liquor was eighteen at that time, but no one ever asked.

Somehow, I had made it through. Somehow, we all make it through. I have never been a day without work since.

Self-Reliance

Listen, don't get me wrong: I am *not* telling everyone to drop out of school. What I am saying is what Mrs. Mundy wisely told my father: "It's not for everybody."

If that's true for you, please don't beat yourself up because you're different. It's okay to be different. Our educational system doesn't work for a whole lot of people, many of whom are artists.

Believe it or not, you don't need a massive education to create a fulfilling and successful life. What you need is to believe in yourself. Know what you want. Know you have inner support, and believe in that, too.

What you need, no matter the degrees or lack of them, is the interest and desire to accomplish something that will *contribute*. You need an answer to the question *If I could have anything in the world, barring all obstacles, what would that be?*

Write *that* script. Write that story. Become an expert by educating *yourself* in the areas *you* choose and in ways you feel fit best.

I promise you, you don't need a fancy, expensive education to create the life of your dreams. You need to be your *own* person and think for yourself. You need to possess a curiosity, a desire, and a willingness to learn. You need to work hard because you *love* to. You need to read often, listen carefully, observe with objectivity, and—most importantly—you need to trust in the authority of your own counsel.

Learning to think for yourself has little to do with education. A person who has learned to think for themselves can stand confidently in their own boots and contribute. A person who has learned to think for themselves is not just a personality seeking the admiration of others, but a human being operating in concert with their own heart.

This person has achieved *self-reliance*, and in so doing, they contribute their unique and powerful frequency to uplifting humanity as the collective energy that we are.

Know this: to successfully navigate a life of our own choosing, we must educate *ourselves*. It's our job!

You are more powerful than you can imagine! Your job as a human being is to awaken to that truth. That's why we're here! Unfortunately, at this particular time in history, traditional education contributes very little to helping an individual to become their own person.

But everything is changing.

Bad Attitude

Attitude is everything!

Let me say that again.

Attitude is everything!

I learned this fact the hard way. As an insecure, angry young woman, I had a pretty gross attitude, and worst of all, I was proud of it. I had a chip on my shoulder that took up the whole room. I had a knee-jerk reaction to *all* authority and was highly suspicious of anyone who took on the mantle of knowing something I didn't. I've been called a "know it all," "haughty," "intimidating," "superior," "prissy," and a whole lot more, I'm sure.

Being "too sensitive," I felt the need to protect myself, so I unconsciously installed a lot of off-putting mannerisms to create distance—then, I'd worry obsessively about why people were put off by me. This is a pretty good example of the Universe reflecting back the *exact* vibration I was projecting.

Actors are sensitive. They experience a lot of rejection; it's part of the job. They become defensive at times and cop crappy attitudes. Their egos rage. No one wants to hire a crappy attitude; you can smell it across the room.

Think about it: have you ever succeeded at anything while indulging in a crappy attitude?

In my early twenties, when I first pursued acting in Los Angeles, I was terribly insecure. I didn't realize it at the time because I was so busy covering it up with arrogance. I hated auditioning because it meant being judged—so I would reverse the positioning and weigh in on the arbiters. Even as I was auditioning for them, I believed the people in the room to be without the artistic pedigree to judge me. My inner thinking was, *Who are you to know anything? You'd like to be an artist, and you're not even trying.* I was filled to the brim with superiority, stemming from unacceptable feelings of inferiority. People reveal themselves in the opposite.

I got a call from my agent one day. "Jocelyn, what the hell are you doing in the room?" he yelled. "If one more person tells me, 'She gave the best reading—we're going another way,' I'm gonna fire you as a client. They're afraid of you, for Chrissake!"

My answer was to put him on the long list of assholes I had to contend with. I was hostile because I couldn't admit (even to myself) how vulnerable and insecure I felt. Putting myself on the line felt like it might just kill me. Vulnerability, I learned, could be channeled into the work, but insecurity? Insecurity was utterly unacceptable. Insecurity felt like a major secret that had to be protected.

But this secret (or not-so-secret) self-doubt ruled me. I was obsessed with worry. What if *this* terrible thing happens—or *that*? I couldn't admit how petrified I was. And because I couldn't accept the truth, I couldn't get beyond it.

Instead of recognizing and accepting my fear, I attended to my ego—protecting myself with false bravado. I'd hang my limbs and cop a cool attitude. *You must be mistaking me for someone who gives a shit.*

Of course, the opposite was true: I cared so much, I agonized 24/7.

Ego doesn't exist without think-think-*thinking*! Here I was, *thinking* all the time about the problems and repercussions of putting myself out there and being rejected. Here I was, trying to pump myself up and protect my ego with *thoughts*. I played out every scenario in my head. *I mean, being rejected is bad; on the other hand, winning could be even more traumatic!* The conflict was paralyzing.

In the end, all this strategy about how to protect myself—how to come out on top, if only in my own mind—and all this *thinking* was completely debilitating. Attending to a bad attitude is all-consuming. Nothing of consequence gets *done!*

Law of Attraction in Action

The first scene I did for Milton Katselas, the acting teacher who would become my first mentor, was a monologue I'd adapted from a 1930's Dorothy Parker short story called "A Telephone Call." A woman, alone in her apartment, is wildly distraught because the man she's dating promised to return her call two hours ago. Through her ongoing conversation with God, we see the depths of her desperation as she pleads with him to intervene in the apparent ghosting by her boyfriend. "It isn't very much to ask. It would be so little to you, God—such a little, little thing. Only let him telephone me now. Please, God?"

It was fairly easy for me to channel my terror and insecurity into the role, but then came the hard part—the critique. My new (super intimidating and loving it) teacher was to pass judgment. I sat on the edge of the stage with my heart in my throat, my mind racing.

"You have a formidable talent," Milton said.

A dramatic opening, I thought. I looked up *formidable* after the critique—it felt like a backhanded compliment. I remember reading the words: *intense, intimidating, inspiring fear.* Odd way to speak about someone's acting, I thought—but okay. I kind of like it.

He went on to say, "Do you know why you're not hired more?"

I looked at him, thinking, *You arrogant guru-fuck! I suppose you're going to tell me* and slammed a protective smile on my face.

"You're just a little bit of a shit," he dropped.

The air went out of the room. Milton had called me a shit to my face, and time stood still as I weighed my choices.

I could walk; I was good at that, and it would be dramatic. I could play disdain, but I was already doing that. Or, I could *talk*—it could be fun to flex my articulation and launch into some hypercritical argument about what a bad teacher he was and why.

I did none of the above. Milton was right—but his in-your-face approach didn't help me. What I needed more than anything was kindness. What I needed was for someone to look past my bad attitude and see the terrified child who ruled me. Then, maybe I could see what he was talking about.

I froze, locked in defensiveness. My vibe was so thick it could break plates. (I've actually broken plates with my vibe, but that's another story.)

Again, I was getting back exactly what I put out. I sat on the edge of the stage (inwardly terrified and defensive) with my arms crossed over my chest, my chin held too high, and my face reflecting my attitude—*Okay big shot, what've you got? And by the way, watch yourself, or I will fucking kill you!*

I'm embarrassed to say I was that bad, but I was. Much of the time, my *thoughts* broadcast blame, righteousness, criticism, and complaint—all indicators of a terrible attitude.

When you think like that, it's like loaning your power to a saboteur. It's like saying, "Here, let me give you this gun so you can shoot me in my left kidney." In other words, you are asking for more of the same.

Because I struggled for so long with my own lousy attitude, it was fairly easy for me to spot the same kind of thinking in my own students later on. "It's poison," I would tell them as I pointed out the importance of becoming aware of the *quality* of their thoughts. "Your negative attitude is guaranteed to isolate you from your heart's desire."

Where the mind goes, energy flows. I'm not sure who first said this because it's attributed to so many—but the sentiment is entirely true. What we *think*, we project. What we project, we *become*. So, it's a good idea for us to gain a little more awareness and control over our thinking and desires.

This is not exactly a new concept; it's been around for centuries. The concept keeps arriving in slightly different variations—this idea that we are responsible for our own reality.

Until we *discover* this for ourselves and take responsibility for our own thinking, we are like a straw in the wind—ruled by our own negativity.

Great Thinkers on the Law of Attraction

"All that we are is a result of what we have thought."
—BUDDHA

"There is nothing either good or bad, but thinking makes it so."
—WILLIAM SHAKESPEARE

"A person is what he or she thinks about all day long."
—RALPH WALDO EMERSON

"When I believe I can, I acquire the ability to do it."
—MAHATMA GANDHI

"Match the frequency of the reality you want and you cannot help but get that reality. This is not philosophy. This is physics."
—ALBERT EINSTEIN

"Whether you believe you can do a thing or not, you are right."
—HENRY FORD

"Change your life by changing your thoughts."
—PARAMAHANSA YOGANANDA

"The positive thinker sees the invisible, feels the intangible, and achieves the impossible."
—WINSTON CHURCHILL

"The more man meditates upon good thoughts, the better will be his world and the world at large."
—CONFUCIUS

The Importance of Personal Discovery

As a teacher, I find artists acutely sensitive. All I have to do is *see* them and acknowledge them for who they really are, and then watch as that recognition empowers them. My intention is to *see* a student at their best, which almost always creates the space for them to rise to the occasion for themselves.

This is a valuable approach to our interactions with anyone in our lives. Imagine if our intention were always to discover *the best* in each other. That tiny shift alone would uplift humanity immeasurably.

In my thirty years of working with actors, I looked for a definition of *art* that rang my bell. I never found one. Definitions included creative skill, beauty, emotional power, imagination, craft, and even cunning. Okay, but what was the bottom line?

For my own purposes, I crafted a simple definition that rings true to me. I tell my students,

"Art is the expression of that which you have personally discovered." It's the joy of discovery that permeates the expression. Personal discovery magically strikes a universal chord.

Without some form of discovery, the work is derivative. Not that I feel derivative work is the enemy—on the contrary, I believe we learn a lot by imitation. But once we gain some technique and get our feet on the ground, it's what we *intend* that counts. I recommend intending *discovery*, and once found, *imagining* a way to express it.

The two simplest roads to discovery are:

1. Ask questions, lots and lots of questions. Then *patiently* wait for the answers. The trick is to keep asking. Don't stop at the first intellectual offerings. Keep asking, "What else? What else could it be?" Ask until you get an answer that vibrates with the unmistakable thrill of something new and exciting! You'll know when you've struck gold because it's visceral—something moves in you.

2. Still yourself and quietly observe without any fixed ideas or judgment. In other words, look at things! Lift your face up out of the screens and become *interested*. Take the time to observe life in an open, nonjudgmental manner until you *discover* your own point of view.

There's no room for judgment in this process. Judgment is a self-imposed prison.

Self cannot be discovered by *thinking* about self. That's ego-tripping. We *discover* self reflected in the things we're interested in *outside* ourselves.

Focusing your interest *outside* yourself gets easier with practice. You can cultivate a high interest in life exactly the way you develop anything else—by putting quality attention on it. By observing and listening fully. By practicing.

Artists focus their interest on people and things outside themselves because they want to *expand* more than they want to be admired.

What is an actor looking for in their work? They're looking for a way into the heart of the character. They're listening for that beat of compassion that bridges their soul to another's. At some point, the actor uncovers such a depth of understanding that their heart begins beating for two. This is what the actor *intends*—this "entry" into character. This *oneness*.

Imagine if we valued this process as human beings. Imagine if we intended to understand the heart of another. Imagine if we treated each other with such interest and care. It's a simple shift in intention— move attention *off* self and *on* to another. *Intend* to understand them.

The more time you spend in the present moment, the higher your vibrational frequency. The higher your vibrational frequency, the more you'll *discover* things that were unavailable to you before. When in consultation with your higher self, life and art begin to develop in a more dynamic direction.

Best of all, you'll begin to learn by *flow and synchronicity* as opposed to hardship and suffering.

Become interested in *everyone*! Become interested in *everything*! From architecture to horticulture; from people's behavior to the language of animals. Read. Walk. Look. Study the classics. Cook a new dish. Spend time alone discovering what interests and excites you. Live! Live without complaint. You are blessed!

Once you *discover* where it is YOU honestly want to go in life, it's easy to plot a road map to get there. Keep in mind: what you don't *know*—you can learn. Learning is all about personal discovery.

Exercise:
Self-Education

Here's an exercise to help you learn a little more about the person you want to become.

Close your eyes, and listen to your breath.

Inhale: I breathe in what I innately know to be true.

Exhale: I open to that which I have yet to see.

After ten minutes, open your eyes. When you are ready, complete the following journal exercise:

- List the five subjects you are most curious about. For example:

  * Photography

  * Script writing

  * Organic gardening

  * Watercolors

  * Sustainable lifestyles

Circle one of the five. You're going to do some self-education on this subject. Consider these resources:

- Books

  * Research and discover three to five books on the topic that pique your interest, and read any reviews you can find. You can also research the authors.

  * In your journal, write about *why* these books captured your interest.

  * Of those books, choose two to start. Buy one as an audio book and one to read. If you are short on funds, your local library has both audio and regular book selections. If they don't have what you want, they will often order the book for you. When choosing audio books, it's helpful to utilize Amazon's free examples so you can hear the reader's voice and make sure you enjoy the sound of it. Audio books double your reading time. I listen to them while I walk.

- Articles

  * Use Google and find five articles of interest on the subject.

  * Copy and paste them into Word documents, and start a file on your subject.

- Pictures

  * Find five images that move you, and copy them into your files.

- Films

  * Make a list of five films on your subject, both fiction
    and documentary. Then, choose your first film to
    watch.

- Expertise

  * Seek out experts you might interview or take
    classes with.

- Hands-On Experience

  * Practice what you can *do* regarding your subject.
    For example, if you are interested in photography,
    you will research photography in all the above
    ways, but you will also take pictures.

- Imagining

  * With everything you know on the subject so far,
    what more can you imagine about it?

  * What *could* be possible?

  * How can you imagine expanding this area of inter-
    est in your life?

In the end, we are developing our own barometer of interest. We are seeking to discover our own point of view. We are
what we practice. Practicing self-education is another way to
expand beyond the limits of your personality.

CHAPTER 10

Waking Up to Joy

"You don't have to see the whole staircase, just take the first step."

—MARTIN LUTHER KING, JR.

ON A COLD DECEMBER NIGHT IN MANHATTAN, I CAME OUT OF A mediocre show at the Shubert on 44th Street, and it was snowing hard. The wind barreled down 8th Avenue and cut right through me as I turned the corner and joined the chorus of other theatergoers screaming, "Taxi!"

Walking backward through traffic, I jockeyed for position, cursing my head off as, one by one, other sharks seemed to grab my cab. Three different times, I tried to cut in front of people in an effort to steal theirs. I had no shame.

I was beside myself with frustration when I was stopped in my tracks by a Salvation Army guy, violently shaking his bell in my face. As he schooled me on my unbecoming behavior, I wrote him off as a run-of-the-mill street crazy and dodged him like he was radioactive.

Pulling my woolly hat down and my collar up, I resigned myself to hoofing it twenty-two blocks home. By the time I got to 53rd

Street, I lifted my head and looked around. Snow collected on my eyelashes as I thought, *Gee, I feel kind of good!*

The wind died down. The snow turned to big, fluffy puffs, and the Christmas lights, reflected in the flurry of it all, seemed downright mystical. By the time I reached 59th Street, I was shivering—freezing cold, but alert and happy! As I took in the city, its radiance emerged, and I decided to change course.

I crossed over to Central Park West, feeling drawn to the white snow on black branches, reminding me of white silk evening gloves on long thin arms, making me think of an Alvin Ailey dance. The park was a study in black and white, and I wondered why I'd never seen it like that before.

I stood at the entrance, struck by the quality of silence. Snow covered everything, softening the sounds of the city. I listened. It sounded like peace.

I looked down a winding path that led deep into the park and saw a lamppost in the distance. The diffuse light swirled around, and the image made me think of Narnia, and Mr. Tumnus, and the magic of books.

I began to think about the play I'd just seen. It wasn't so bad. Actually, it was ambitious, tackling themes seldom dealt with before. Though it wasn't completely successful, I could see the intention to break new ground. It had impact. I didn't necessarily *like* the play, but it got me thinking and made me *feel*.

It was original. In fact, there may have been a seed of genius in there somewhere.

We need to take risks more often, I thought. *Artists need to fail, get up, and try again. Like much of life, we need our failures to point us in the direction of success.* I considered the mediocrity of much of today's "entertainment" and wondered how it got that way.

I thought of the malicious judgment that proliferates our lives and art these days. *How is one to take a leap of faith when there is an army of executioners waiting to hack us to death with their mean-spirited opinions? If we pander to the approval of internet trolls, are we not doomed to mediocrity?*

What is a culture of hate, if not a lost tribe of people living in fear? How do we lift ourselves up to a higher standard? How do we inspire people to reach for the best in humanity as opposed to cannibalizing it?

Is it possible to challenge artists with the job of dissolving fear in people's hearts by lifting them up to a higher perspective? If not the artists, then who?

My own bad behavior and the Salvation Army guy came to mind. I *was* trying to steal a cab, and I didn't care who saw it. But *he* did. I wanted a cab in the worst way and copped a superior attitude, believing I was entitled. *He* didn't. And he was determined to get that point across to me. *Hmmmm? Are these not the actions of someone who cares about you, holding you to a higher standard?*

I looked at what happened in a new light, realizing he'd given me a gift. Encountering him was a *gesture*, like a sudden breeze whispering in my ear. Only in this case, it was a giant bell screaming, "WAKE UP!"

Was he a Salvation Army man? Or was he some form of *angel* trying to shake me out of my unbecoming coma? If I'd turned around, would he still have been there? Or would he be gone? Mission accomplished.

I looked back through the park. The snow had stopped, and a full moon slipped from behind a cloud, spilling light on the frosted trees. It was exquisite! Tears came as I took in the scene. Gratitude overwhelmed me, for the man with the bell who'd sent me there. I breathed into it, realizing I was experiencing a peak moment.

I wanted to freeze time, wishing I could live my whole life from that perfect perspective.

What happened here? I WOKE UP!

I was *fully* in the moment and recognizing the miracle that is life. I was filled to the brim with beauty. And love. And so much gratitude. I was awake, connected to spirit, and feeling like my very best self. And oh, how I longed to stay in that state.

That's the question, isn't it? How? How do we *stay* awake?

Awakening

Life is either happening *to* you, and you feel victim to it, or *you* are happening to your life.

To consciously create your own life, you have to stay awake! So, the question becomes: how do we stay awake? How do we listen to our heart, make worthwhile choices, and select our most beneficial actions?

The trick is to break free from the relentless *thinking* that fortifies the *small* self—and instead enter the moment of NOW, where the *higher self* resides.

Sometimes, you fill the heart with a single breath, and you're there. Other times, you have to surrender, as if you allow the present moment to enter you—through breath. As if you are *being* breathed.

However you reach that sacred place, once there, time expands, the birds sing more clearly, the skies shine more brightly, and nature calls out to you—*look at me, look at me, look at me!*

As you admire the beauty of your favorite tree, taking her in without so much as a label, opening to that which you've never seen—your *energies* merge. And through the power of your admiration, the tree takes a leap of consciousness, too—her sacred beauty acknowledged for perhaps the first time in all her existence. As if she's waited her whole life for you to *see* her.

Nature is longing to communicate with us. We are meant to find our commonality, that silent *beingness* that connects us in a different but expansive interaction.

Observing nature. Meditation. Falling in love with the mundane. Breath work. These are all *practices* that support living in the here and now. Often the trick is just to START. My students once made a bumper sticker with a saying I often used in class: "Do it anyway!"

When you *don't* want to do a thing, even though you *know* it's the best choice in the moment, just go ahead and *do it anyway*! One foot in front of the other. Like Gracie taught me, count off. One step, two steps, three…and done!

"Do it anyway" is a great habit to develop. You're bypassing procrastination's three best friends: thinking, debating, and psychoanalyzing.

When you do the thing you know is best for you, even though you don't really want to—you are immediately grateful you did. It's an instant morale booster, like you won something. You did! You won your own free will.

The human *being* is so fast by nature that once we *see* a destination, we think we're entitled to bypass steps one through one hundred to get there. We focus on our frustration and whine about how long it will take—which, of course, makes it take longer. Sometimes, we just need to get on with it and trust that the fastest way to get there is to simply take the steps, give it our best, and *enjoy* the journey!

Otherwise, we are working *against* ourselves. Blaming, complaining, and indulging in self-pity are all well-known forms of soul-crushing self-sabotage. They're a complete waste of time and only attract more reasons to perpetuate and justify the same crappy attitude.

In an age when dishonesty rages, the rehabilitation of truth begins with the individual. Within each of us lives a universal truth. We have only to practice *being* here to hear, feel, and know it.

Each and every one of us *knows* what's best for us. We know how to do the right thing. We know how to be kind to ourselves and others. We simply need to practice those things until they become our customary behavior.

Imagining

When I greet my students at the top of class, I sense in them an eagerness to *see* something, *feel* something, and *know* something they didn't see, feel, or know before. They're aware that humanity is only scratching the surface, and they want more. They want techniques that will help them land acting jobs, but more importantly, they want a rewarding life!

And they want examples. What do people creating a rewarding life look like, act like, live like? What can they do to find this situation for themselves?

I want them to make an adjustment—I want them to ask themselves the big question: *if I could have anything in the world, barring all obstacles, what would that be?*

I want them to still themselves, take a breath, and direct the question within. And I want them to keep asking the same question until they *imagine* an answer that excites them.

If I could have anything in the world, barring all obstacles, what would that be?

Keep asking. Journal about it. Give it a week or so. Give it a lifetime. Keep asking. Keep writing. Keep *imagining* until you feel the quickening of your own heart.

When the "aha" moment arrives—and it will—draw a picture of it in great detail. Write it down. Sketch it. Use colored pens, watercolors, or simply words—and keep it in a vision book of goals you're consciously manifesting.

Albert Einstein famously said, "The true sign of intelligence is not knowledge but imagination."

We need to honor and care for our imaginations. Imagination is the collaboration between the desires of the Universe and our own personal experience.

Imagining is the midwife of possibility. Imaginative visualization is the instrument of manifestation. We invite imagination into our lives by asking questions. What *could* it be? How *might* it go? How might I contribute?

Humans LOVE pictures! We love pictures so much that we've become addicted to them. We need to be mindful of the pictures we take in.

This is how advertisers hijack our attention: they hook us with glossy pictures. They play to our subconscious and the lower frequencies of fear, vanity, greed, competition, and selfishness. Dark pictures stimulate dark imaginings and make up dark realities. But they sell! Media has way more influence over us than is healthy. But we can easily put media in check—just turn it off.

When we read, listen to stories, and daydream, we exercise our imagination by creating our *own* pictures. When screens of all kinds *deliver* us pictures, we bypass that important exercise and weaken our ability to imagine. We get lazy. Like unexercised muscles, the best part of our mind atrophies. We want things delivered to us.

Rather than engaging in life and discovering our passions through participation, we become mesmerized by—and addicted to—someone else's pictures.

This is why we have a problem with illiteracy today: too many screens delivering too many pictures. This state of affairs steals a reader's ability to *imagine* and replaces it with the expectation and desire for a life delivered.

When people can't *imagine* a life of purpose for themselves, they become ripe for enslavement. But that's another story.

We do well when the pictures we entertain ourselves with come from our own imagination. This is why reading is so enriching. When we read, we create our *own* pictures. We *see* and imagine things as our own person. We *exercise* our imagination. When five people read the same novel, they see five different movies in their mind's eye.

Know this: when you inhibit imagination, you inhibit art. You inhibit a person's ability to think for themselves. You inhibit discovery. You inhibit possibility. You inhibit greatness.

Conversely, if you imagine yourself doing it, being it, and having it—and take steps toward it every day exactly as if it were already yours—it *will* be yours!

To manifest a life of your dreams, you need only to care for and cultivate your own imagination.

We are energetic beings in bodies, and we are at a crossroads. Do we reach for our full potential as human beings? Or do we evolve into something more akin to the robots we engage with daily?

Seeking Joy

Babies arrive in their natural state, tiny bundles of joy. They bring the gifts of love and truth. They come to remind us that life is a miracle, and they search our faces to see if they've accomplished their mission. They are looking for their effect on us. Do your eyes shine with love? Does your smile reflect the joy they've brought you? They measure your attention with perfect accuracy—an accuracy that will fade over the years as they shift from *being* in present time to *worrying*, a big component of *thinking* too much.

A split second before we arrive to embody yet another individual consciousness, we remind ourselves: *Never forget who you are. Never forget why you agreed to come again. Never forget what you know.*

And then, BAM! We arrive—feeling like we ran into the side of a mountain in a 747 to get here. And in an instant, we forget everything! We forget *who* we are, *what* we are, and *why* we came.

We have contracts when we come into the world, which we also forget when we're born. Sometimes, our parents supply the love and support we need to easily thrive and grow—sometimes not. Sometimes, the faces we look up at in those first few days, months, and years are so lost in their own unhappiness that they don't even see us.

When a baby can't bring a smile to their mother's eyes, they internalize the problem. They feel, *There must be something wrong with me. I have failed to bring joy.* Eventually, they abandon the effort and look for comfort elsewhere. Often, they become lonely, distant, and lost.

Our purpose as human beings is simple: we're here to bring joy to ourselves and those around us. Joy vibrates at the same level as creation. You were born to *create* your own life. You were born to create out of *joy.*

We may have a rough beginning, something to really push against. Then later in life, we feel hurt and lost due to our circumstances. We certainly don't remember any contract. "Contract for growth? Are you crazy? Do you think I would wish this on myself?"

This is the narrative of the victim. Life is happening *to* them. They're not creating it; they feel they have no control. They are stuck in the past, trying to fix something that isn't there anymore. Sometimes, our circumstances are so brutal that they feel impossible to overcome. Whatever our conditions growing up, they are the makeup of our *story*—the story we polish up to excuse ourselves and justify our limitations, when in truth, we have none. But we *are* what we *believe.* And we will seek evidence to prove it.

I tell my students the truth is multifaceted—and we will *see* only as much as we're willing to act on. Conversely, if we *decide* we're willing to take responsibility for what we discover, then we'll *see* more truth in any given situation.

This is why it's wise to observe, stay open, acknowledge what we perceive—and then look for what it is we're still *not* seeing. When we observe without judgment, we arrive in the moment, open and ready to *expand.*

Happiness vs. Joy

I think of happiness as happening to us. Something unexpected and wonderful occurs. We win a prize. We receive good news. Someone we admire sees us or validates us.

Happiness is like a shot of adrenaline to the heart.

The nervous system ignites with delight and dances about in celebration.

Depending on the magnitude of the happy event, our cheerfulness might stick around for hours or even days.

Joy, on the other hand, is the practice of acceptance and the cultivation of beauty.

It is a victorious breath that fills the heart with an exquisite feeling of peace.

It is knowing how to center in the midst of a storm by returning home on a wave of air.

Happiness visits us for a time.

Joy, on the other hand, can become an integral part of our daily life.

Happiness is often loud.

Joy is quiet and blissfully still.

We *share* our happiness.

We *are* our joy.

I teach people to create out of joy. I do not subscribe to the idea that the best artists create out of pain and unhappiness.

You can discover joy by doing the things you love, doing them often, and doing them with extra care.

You can cultivate joy by discovering beauty in the mundane tasks of everyday life, such as savoring the hot soapy water when you wash the dishes or admiring the herbs from the garden as you sprinkle them over the omelet you just made.

Joy lives in the four o'clock light sliding through the window, spilling across the floor, and caressing the cat with its heat.

Joy is at the heart of every grateful moment, as gratitude and joy walk hand in hand.

It's easy to see why we've been brainwashed into believing *money* is the answer to happiness. Money is security. Money buys us *things*. Things are fun. Surely fun must be the road to joy.

People are following the money when they should be on the lookout for a *feeling* inside.

People are seeking answers all over the place these days. We consult astrologers, buy crystals, read oracle cards, and throw the I Ching.

There are healers who see our chakras, move our energy about, and clear us with feathers. We are longing for answers and seek definitive explanations from any authority—even as everything we need is right there inside us.

The answers are simple, but we live in such a complex world that simplicity has become difficult to access. We don't believe it. Can it really be that simple?

The answer is *yes*. The truth is always simple; it's lies that are complicated. The truth is:

> *The past is gone*

> *The future doesn't exist*

> *There is only NOW*

The truth is we've lost our predilection for doing what we innately know to be right.

To practice kindness toward our fellow human beings. To tell the truth even when inconvenient. To *participate* and create—rather than disappearing into the masses as one more bystander.

Time for a new paradigm. Time to take counsel from our own heart, rather than what we're being "influenced" to buy and believe.

> *Time to slow down and* breathe...

> *One slow, deep, connecting breath*

> *Inhale—nice*

Exhale—let it all go

There...there's my heart

Let me just rest here in my breath and listen to my heart

Focused observation, starting with our own breath, is where we find ourselves—the observer.

That exquisite invisible energy that is our heart and soul. The witness. Awareness. Presence.

> *It is possible to cultivate joy in the fundamental activities of our lives*
>
> *It is possible to move through our day with gratitude as opposed to complaint*
>
> *It is possible to practice the art of living*
>
> *It's personal*
>
> *It is a living meditation*
>
> *It is a connection to our higher selves*
>
> *WE are consciousness seeking to witness and reflect what is*

Where you live, how you eat, who you love, how you treat yourself and others, how you spend your time and money—are you making conscious choices in the details of these basics? Are you actively engaged in the creation of your own life? Are you seeking joy?

If not, it's time to wake up to what is possible for you. And you know what? My guess is, it's more than you have ever imagined.

Joy List

Actors worry! They pretty much worry about everything—all the time. Worry creates a serious outlook. A serious outlook is never *fun*. It's hard to create when there's no fun around. Joy and creativity go hand in hand. I don't think it's possible to have one without the other.

I worked with an actor for years who had a big career on a long-running TV series. Like all hit shows, eventually, it was canceled, and he spent the next ten years of his life chasing that high. He bounced around the TV circuit doing a number of less successful series, but I spotted his unhappiness and felt compelled to chat with him about it.

There was a heaviness about him, a sadness. I sensed it was holding him back and affecting his appeal. I took in his appearance. His face was puffy. *Uncried tears and alcohol,* I thought. He's a handsome man, but he'd cut his hair too short. *Did someone tell him it would make him look younger?*

When we chatted, I discovered he had been separated from his wife for many years but still lived in the house they'd shared together. He was surrounded by her things, still hurting, and he was unwilling to let it all go. He seemed stuck. Further, he was drinking too much and sleeping with anything in a skirt.

I suggested he slow down on the drinking, stop screwing around, and grow his hair out. He was a leading man after all—and, like Clint Eastwood, he would be a leading man until the end of time!

I recommended he confront the situation with his wife and have her take her stuff out of the house so he could reclaim his space.

Most importantly, I asked him to make a "joy list," a list of activities that brought him joy, and share it with me.

It took him a week to get one thing on the list—golf. But after confronting it every day, he slowly started to remember not only things he loved to do but also things he was interested in learning more about.

Within six months, he had grown his hair out, lost the boozy bloat, and booked a terrific job. A year and a half later, he'd not only gotten his wife's things out of his house but also divorced her, sold the place, met another woman, married her—and had his first child! Plus, he was working more than ever.

Bonus Exercise: Joy List

Knowing what you love, doing those things, and doing them often is a way to bring more joy into your life. It's a way of lifting your spirit. It's a way to nurture your soul.

Close your eyes and breathe into your heart.

Inhale: I breathe in joy—I smile.

Exhale: I offer my heart to the world.

Expand your inner space with each inhalation. After ten minutes, open your eyes.

- Make a list of things that bring you joy. Start with five. Keep adding to your list until you get to ten or more.

- Chose something from your list to experiment with. Add it to your calendar, and do this activity at least two times in the upcoming week.

- Write about your experience in your journal.

- Choose another activity or two for the upcoming week, and do the same.

Your joy list is a place from which dreams and visions are born. Add to your list, subtract from it, journal about it. Seek out new things, and be open to them. *Choosing* to do things you enjoy is an exercise in lifting your vibration at will.

If you find yourself having trouble with this assignment, and I know plenty of people do, try this: find some quiet time to reflect on the things in your *past* that made you come alive. Things that brought you excitement. Activities you used to look forward to. Maybe it was a pottery class you took in high school. Or playing in your mother's garden as a child. Maybe it was winning the softball tournament or cooking with your grandmother. Maybe it's playing golf, writing short stories, painting, listening to music, dancing like no one is watching. Maybe it is simply walking in the park.

You catch my drift? Write down whatever applies: pottery, gardens, softball, writing, painting, cooking, golf, music, dancing, walking in the park.

Explore *these* things! See what's still alive for you. Incorporate these things into your life, even if they seem out of your comfort zone now—especially if they feel out of your comfort zone! Just *start*! If you don't have space for a garden, get a pot of fresh mint to put in your window. If you don't have a window, move.

I promise you if you join a softball league in your area, one of two things will happen: you will resurrect a past love and meet new people who feel equally enthusiastic about playing, or you'll discover softball's no longer your thing and move on to the next item on the list.

There is such a thing as sense memory. For an actor, this means if you drink a glass of water and treat it *exactly* as if it were vodka— pouring just the right amount into the glass, listening to it hit the ice, imagining the burn at the back of the throat, the acidic feeling as it slides down and hits your stomach—if you loan your belief to the details of the water *as if* it were vodka, you'll begin to get a buzz. The body says, *Oh, yeah—the clink of the ice, the smell of the lemon, the burn, the acid,* and fills in the sensory component.

Your body and mind *remember* what it's like to be filled with joy. You have only to remember what brought about those feelings and *do* those things to get you started in the right direction.

Actors worry about crying on cue. I tell them, "Assume the position. Begin by doing the things you do when you cry." I want them to behave like a real person in their acting—not just show us what they *think* it looks like. "Try not to cry," I tell them. Actors try to cry on cue, while most people try very hard *not* to cry. *Do the things you do to keep from crying, and you will stimulate real tears.*

Assume the position of happiness. Smile, and you'll soon have something to smile about. By seeking out joy in tried-and-true activities, you are more likely to invite joy into the ordinary tasks of your day-to-day living, allowing you to live your life more artfully.

Joy comes together like the sea, one drop at a time.

Exercise:
Enhancing Your Ability to Stay Awake

Here's a review of the things you can practice to stay awake and consciously create the life you were born to live:

- Take a walk outside. Observe and listen to nature. Discover her beauty. Breathe it in.

- Look at the space between forms.

- Listen to the sounds between sounds.

- Observe the detailed behavior in your mundane daily tasks—making coffee, brushing teeth, washing dishes. *Be* there and enjoy.

- Take in the energy of the plants as you prepare meals. Think about where they were grown and the farmers who nurtured them. Be grateful for their offerings. Admire them! *All* living things respond to admiration.

- See if you can make the people you love laugh every day.

- See if you can make a stranger smile.

- Practice listening to others. Listen without judgment. Ask questions. Really take in their answers. *Be* in present time.

- Play! Create something every day! Even if it's breakfast or a bouquet of flowers—make something beautiful every day.

- Still yourself several times a day, and take a moment to be grateful for the extraordinary bounty life has to offer.

Staying awake is like toning your muscles. Like all exercise, with practice and persistence, we become stronger and more able. We are what we practice.

When I look back, I realize my walk home in the snow after the theatre that night turned into meditation at some point. When I noticed the beauty of the park and decided to cross the street and take it in, I was wide awake! Part of a peak moment is that we feel more *awake* than ever.

But what if I'd been awake when I first bumped into the guy from the Salvation Army? Might I have seen him in a different light? Might I have greeted him as a fellow traveler?

CHAPTER 11

Tales from Hollywood

"Storytelling is the most powerful way to put ideas into the world."

—ROBERT MCKEE

FROM THE FIRST TIME I LIVED WITH MY FATHER AT TOPANGA BEACH, until his final years when we lived together once again—this time with my husband and daughter in Santa Monica—he took great pleasure in going out to dinner. When work was going well, he liked to celebrate with a fine dining experience. When work was in a slump, he liked to discover some hole-in-the-wall, mom-and-pop shop that served family recipes dating back generations. One of Henry's signature moves was to ask the chef to serve us what *they'd* like to prepare. Smart move—chefs love that. We had some memorable dining experiences with that order.

Actors are storytellers, and my father told a tale like the best of them—epic stories about life in the theatre and lots of tales from Hollywood.

Hollywood, after all, was ground zero for storytelling. Parties, gossip, wondrous events, places to see and be seen—all grist for the storytelling mill. As a young teen, my father had taken me to dinner parties at the homes of stars, studio events with hundreds

195

of people milling about, and lunches at the Beverly Hills Hotel's Polo Lounge, where the maître d' knew my father by name. That was a big deal back then. Little did I know my own storytelling reserves were growing with each and every experience my father shared with me.

For instance, my father was a favorite of Alfred Hitchcock and had worked for him in both television and film. He had famously delivered the longest monologue of its time at the end of *Vertigo*, playing the coroner. Because of their connection, not only did I have the privilege of watching Hitchcock direct, I also had the honor of accompanying my father to a birthday party being thrown for "Hitch" at Chasen's restaurant. I was fourteen years old at the time, trying to pass for forty.

Chasen's was quintessential Hollywood. Having opened for business in 1936, it was the site of the Academy Awards party for many years. The celebrities who made Chasen's what it was included the likes of Frank Sinatra, Grace Kelly, James Stewart, Ingrid Bergman—the list was endless, and many of these people were at Hitchcock's birthday party that night.

Being surrounded by that many famous faces was dizzying! After a while, even the tuxedo-clad waiters started looking familiar. When my father introduced me to Cary Grant, I almost passed out. There he was, all six-foot-two of him! He wore a tuxedo, relaxed limbs, and that smile. And when he took my hand and said, "Hel-lo, Jo-cel-yn," with more syllables than I imagined possible, he about ruined me for all other men.

In those early days at the beach, as a fourteen-year-old, hormonal, rebel-brat know-it-all—I was acutely aware that my father was trusting me not to embarrass him at these events. He even seemed proud of me. I had never experienced someone being proud of me before.

I rose to the occasion of my best self because Henry was the first person I remember treating me with genuine respect. He not only saw the best in me but also set an example of dignity, decency, and grace. Plus, he was funny! Like Gracie, Henry made me laugh 'til it hurt. He had a wonderful way with language, and restaurants became his "stage."

We talked while he drove to dinner. We talked while we ate. And we talked on the way home. I loved it, and my dad knew I loved it. He seemed to take real pleasure in seeing me have a good time. He would ask me questions, and I would watch in amazement as he listened with real interest to whatever it was I was saying. I felt *seen* as a person for the first time. I felt loved, valued, and like I just might have something to offer.

Getting to know my father grown-up to "grown-up" was a healing experience for me. Along with lots of entertaining stories about his time in the theatre, we also talked about philosophy and spirituality. Mostly, I spoke from the point of view of a young, smartass kid— critical of just about everything. But in me, Henry saw *himself* at that age. He listened with compassion, careful not to crush an emerging process. My father seemed to understand that teenagers sometimes fall into unbecoming behavior in order to discover what they want and *don't* want in their lives.

I remember a particularly long tale he told at a restaurant—right after I was kicked out of Happy Valley boarding school for sneaking out with the twenty-seven-year-old jailbird-creep on a motorcycle.

The night started out icy. I sat with my arms crossed over my chest—nothing to say. I was completely shut down with shame and embarrassment, even as we sat at one of my favorite restaurants. My dad began talking. And he talked, and talked—and suddenly I realized I knew so little about him.

First of all, he'd had a wife before my mother! What?! This certainly distracted me from my sullen self. Her name was Yvonne. She was a world-class pianist and beautiful, and she died from an infected toenail. It was during the war. Penicillin had *just* been discovered and was only available to elites in the military. She got sepsis and died. They had been married less than a year. It was the saddest story I'd ever heard, and I don't think Henry ever recovered. I later found a picture of him on their wedding day—a 1930's bon vivant in a cutaway and a top hat. There is a joy about him—in his smile. I never saw that smile in the life he lived without Yvonne. Instead, there was a hole clear through his heart. What a loss.

He also talked about his parents, whom, I suddenly realized, I knew nothing about. He came from a formal Philadelphia upbringing. His father, John Frances Xavier Jones (I love his name), had been the chief of surgery at two hospitals and came home smelling of anesthesia, which no one in the household enjoyed. My grandmother used to make him bathe before he could see her. Sometimes he'd comply. Sadly, he died before I was born.

My grandmother was Catholic, and her greatest pride was that the cardinal had come to dinner. He'd even graced her table more than once! That was a big deal, evidently. My father went on to say he was sent exclusively to Catholic schools, which he hated—including a boarding school in Canada, where they spoke *only* French and the priests couldn't (or wouldn't) believe he didn't. Most of his education sounded agonizing, but he'd found a way to through.

With the intimate memories he shared that night, Henry drew me away from my personal nightmare by painting me a picture of his own turbulent years. From his formal Catholic upbringing—to the pain of being excommunicated for divorcing my mother, who wanted to marry her lover, who just happened to be my best friend's father. I suddenly saw my father in a new, very human light—like a friend.

Something welled up in me as I experienced his pain. I was captivated by the injustice he'd endured. I ended up far, far away from the humiliation of my boarding school debacle. In a stroke of lovely storytelling, Henry let me know he didn't enjoy his time in school any more than I did—but he got through. He also told me I had nothing to be ashamed of and that I'd get through, too.

He had found a way, with his gift of storytelling, to save me from disgrace.

New York Stories—a Learning Path

Given my history with actors and acting, it might come as a surprise that I tried very hard *not* to become an actor.

After quitting school at seventeen, I left home, moved to Manhattan, crashed at a friend's apartment, and lied about my age so I could work as a waitress at too many 2nd Avenue pubs. This was a standard paradigm for young twenty-somethings starting out in the big city; I was just a few years early to the game.

We'd sometimes pack three or four girls into a one-bedroom apartment, so we could pay our rent and have a little money left over for food and adventure. And then, somewhere in that first year of emancipation, Eileen Ford "discovered" me.

The Ford Modeling Agency was a big deal at the time. I looked a little like Twiggy, who was a sensation back then—but as it turned out, I was a pretty bad model. I didn't like being in front of a camera.

Being peered at through a black box made me feel creepy—like my skin was on inside out.

Eileen would send me out for "test shots," which meant free pictures from highly sexed photographers who would use up-and-coming models to try out new equipment. Almost all of them implored me to take off my blouse because "it would make me look more vulnerable." It was the '60s, and the film *Blow-Up* had just come out—an iconic thriller that rocked the modeling world at a time when half the population was under thirty years old, and the "counterculture" and "free love" were thriving.

After my first round of testing, I brought the pictures back to Eileen. Instead of choosing some for my portfolio, I remember she winced. "Jocelyn, it looks like they lined your family up against the wall and shot them! Too tragic! Too sad! Nobody calls me up and says, 'I want the sad girl,' for Chrissake! You have to do better, dear."

I tried getting comfortable in front of the camera, but I found it to be an intrusive experience. I felt as if the lens could see clear through me to my deepest insecurities. Still, I liked Eileen. She had seen something in me, and because of that, I wanted to do better. So, I convinced her I could.

Out of sheer desperation, I started to create characters with full-on life stories. I needed some *other* persona I could hide behind while in front of the camera. Maybe *I* couldn't enjoy the experience, but Zelda (my alter ego) could.

I took "Zelda's" pictures back to Eileen. "Oh! You're an actor," she said.

"No, not really," I protested. "My dad's an actor. I think one of those in the family is enough."

Eileen ignored me. I booked the first acting job she sent me out on. I played a heroin addict, perfect for the sad girl.

I thought if I was going to act, I ought to study. The Neighborhood Playhouse was supposed to be the best, so I enrolled in its two-year program and worked with Sandy Meisner.

I found Sandy to be tired, without joy, and bored with the subject. Then again, I was very judgmental. Trash talk had been an unfortunate part of my upbringing. In fact, if you were clever about putting others down, it was celebrated. My people were critical of everything. Gossiping behind each other's backs was an obsession in my family and hurtful to all.

Everyone learns in their own time that cutting off the heads of others only *appears* to make us look taller. But we learn by example, and this lowly grab at one-upmanship is so contagious, I still practice daily to uproot the last vestiges. Unless you've learned by example to appreciate the vast differences between us, it takes mindful intention to accept others without labeling, evaluating, or judging them.

Empowered by the arrogance of youth and bored with Mr. Meisner, I started to pontificate on what I thought he *should* be teaching. I held court around our coffee table with my roommates and our Playhouse friends. I did a lot of talking—too much talking and not enough listening, a lifelong lesson of mine. Too much personality and not enough BEING. Too much attention on self and story, and not enough interest in others.

I was arrogant and haughty, and although I had found a way to garner attention, I was still the insecure, sad girl underneath it all. That said, beneath the struggles of my fragile ego was an honest interest in understanding how artistry works and the nature of the artist's influence on humanity.

I didn't last long at the Neighborhood Playhouse. It was an undramatic departure. I lost interest and stopped showing up for classes. When I cavalierly waltzed into rehearsals for the final production of *Splendor in the Grass* (I was cast as Juanita, the high school floozy) two days late, someone asked, "What are you doing here? We recast your part."

I bumbled around the city, moving from apartment to apartment. I waitressed, booked some commercials, acted in a play here and there. After a few years of memory-making, I tired of all the beautiful sadness and left for Los Angeles. I needed a change of environment. I wanted to start a new story.

LA Stories—a Teacher's Path

In LA, I studied with Lee Strasberg, renowned teacher of the Group Theatre, the Actors Studio, and, of course, Marilyn Monroe. Both Lee and Sandy were at the end of their game and seemed tired of it all. Lee was intrigued with psychoanalysis and brought it into the work in ways I found unhealthy. Plus, we'd sit in straight-backed chairs and do sensory work for hours. I remember working on *feeling* sunshine for an hour and a half—which, let's face it, is not for everyone. I love sensory work but feel there are much less arduous ways to enter that world.

Other than that, Lee was a superb director. He gave notes that made you think and offered concepts you could apply to future projects.

I remember after working on the title role in *Antigone*, he said to me, "You just buried your brother with your bare hands—where is the dirt under your nails?" Forever after, I considered the physical elements of a scene in more detail, looking for opportunities to concretize both the inner and outer life of my characters.

Lee also helped me see the polarities of human nature. He talked about the pathology of characters, which opened my eyes to both the light and the dark in us all.

Working with polarities, I discovered that people at their most vulnerable reveal themselves by pretending the opposite of how they actually feel. Highly sensitive people act tough in order to cover their fear. People who obsessively worry about what others think may lead with an air of indifference, as if to say, *You must be confusing me with someone who cares.* Meanwhile, they care desperately. The angry hide their rage behind chillingly convincing smiles. Even when in love, people might act apathetic because they can't bear the idea of rejection.

People lie and feign the opposite to protect themselves. It's nothing new. It's the stuff of epic storytelling and an important detail to consider for anyone interested in human nature. Recognizing this in ourselves and others, and practicing a kindhearted understanding for the unexpressed injuries that lie beneath, is an exercise in compassion.

A few years later, I met the man who had the greatest influence on me as both actor and teacher. Milton Katselas was brilliant and savage in equal measure. I studied with Milton for many years and taught for him for many more. I don't believe we were ever in the same room without provoking each other. Our egos engaged. It was rough at times, but Milton saw the teacher in me, and for that, I am eternally grateful.

Milton seemed to have taken from all those who came before him and created an exceptionally workable, meat-and-potatoes acting technique. His method uses a series of questions designed to help the actor connect to the material in a personal way. I still refer to Milton's techniques in my teaching. They work.

Sandy, Lee, Milton—these men were giants in their field and had equally gigantic egos. They were old-school male authority figures. They were gurus. Even as they pooh-poohed the cult-like adoration they received, you could see they enjoyed it.

All three men taught me that a certain amount of storytelling is necessary when you teach, simply to hold the room's attention. I learned teaching is a delicate balance between the intimate work with the artist in front of you and crafting their lesson in a way that can impinge on the other fifty actors in the room.

Creative Consulting

I started teaching for Milton when I was thirty-seven years old. I'd just had a baby and thought teaching and motherhood went well together. Although I'd had a rewarding career in films and theatre, teaching *called* to me. It seemed to be a role I'd been preparing for my whole life.

After teaching for Milton for more than a decade, I started getting calls from actors who wanted me to coach them privately on projects. Some of them had been students prior; some came by word of mouth. Before I knew it, I'd become a confidential creative consultant to a number of A-list movie stars. I had to stop teaching classes in order to fulfill the demand from private clients.

I'd rehearse with these superstars for hours a day, developing their notes over a period of months. Their scripts went into binders with the scenes on the right, corresponding notes on the left. I would bring them exciting research relating to both subject and character. Sometimes, I'd write bits of their inner dialogue to give them a head start on the character's inner thinking. I loved finding physical behavior that looked great on film and helped tell their story without words. I worked the technique as if I were playing the part myself and adapted my discoveries to suit the star. I did the work they either didn't have time to do or weren't trained to go after. When they could *see* their work organized in the various books I made them, it gave them that much more confidence. And when they could see those notes work on the screen, they would ask for more of my time.

The job kept growing. Eventually, I was traveling to locations, watching dailies, liaising with department heads, script-doctoring, preparing the star for interviews, and developing future projects. I've enjoyed some of the coolest artistic collaborations imaginable, but due to nondisclosure agreements, I cannot cite a one.

What I didn't know at the time was that I'd be on call 24/7—so, after seven years, I felt I'd had enough of all that and took a year off to reflect and recalibrate.

One day I wrote in my journal, "Why would I serve only one when I could serve a hundred?"

I realized this was the same reasoning I employed to set aside my *own* acting career and dedicate myself to teaching. It seemed to apply to my movie-star situation as well. I had the thought *Maybe I should go back to teaching ongoing classes again?*

Milton had died a few years earlier. I don't believe my husband, Miles, and I would have opened our own acting studio while Milton was still alive. Acting teachers are oddly territorial. He would have considered my striking out on my own as disloyal. It would have hurt him, and I chose to respect that at the time.

When we did finally open the Jocelyn Jones Acting Studio, I interviewed every student personally to accomplish the following:

- I wanted to put together a collection of students with a wide age range, all levels of experience, and lots of cultural diversity—as if I were casting players for a theatre company rather than a class.

- I wanted individuals who possessed certain qualities—first and foremost, desire! Next, I was interested in a solid work ethic and, finally, a healthy attitude.

- I wanted to deliver a solid technique that gave actors *certainty* regarding how to successfully approach a project and flush out the opportunities from start to finish.

- I wanted to hone their abilities as actors but also challenge them to expand as people.

I think a teacher's job is to guide and inspire, not come from on high. It is my experience that authoritative teachers who have cult-like followings have usurped their students' power to some degree. A clean and respectful relationship, one whose sole purpose is to empower the *student*, requires consistent attention and care.

Even with these strong intentions, I sometimes failed. We all do. It's how we learn. Everything is a practice.

I am honored to have worked with a great many students over the years. Each has taught me at least as much as I've imparted. I am deeply grateful for that history.

It is through my work as a teacher that I came to believe *anyone* can take control of their life and curate it with guidance from their higher self. This innate truth is what calls to me.

Henry's Final Gift

During the last seven years of my father's life, we lived together under one roof—my father, my husband, my daughter, and I. As always, Henry's greatest pleasure was to take the family out to dinner and tell stories. There was a local French restaurant, where our daughter, Samantha, discovered duck à l'orange—a dish Henry had introduced me to as a child and a favorite of mine. "The apple doesn't fall far from the tree," he mused.

As he encouraged Sam to order it, I watched the pride well up in him. "It's important to make memories, Sammy," he instructed. "The better the memories, the better the stories you have to share." So we did. The four of us made some happy memories together in that tender period of time.

During his last few weeks on Earth, as my father lay dying in his bed, I'd hold his hand and wonder how I might ease the transition for him. He wasn't talking much; his stories were tucked away for now. I'd ask a question, and it might take two or three minutes before he'd answer. Often, he wouldn't answer at all—he was either sleeping or simply disinterested.

Since Henry had recently told me he felt Catholicism was something he'd never successfully extricated from his life, I asked him one morning if he might like to talk to a priest.

"GOD, NO!" came the answer, louder and stronger than I'd expected.

I immediately retreated. "Okay. No problem. Sorry to ask, Pops."

I sat with him in silence, determined not to broach the subject again. But before I knew it, out of my mouth came, "Jonesy?" I sometimes called him that. "Do you believe you are a spirit, or your body, or your brain?" I asked.

He didn't answer for so long I thought he'd either fallen asleep or was deliberately ignoring me.

Then suddenly he said, "Brain. Probably, brain."

"Hmmmm," I answered, not knowing where to go from there.

After another long silence, he asked, "You're a spiritual person—what do you think?" His eyes were closed, but I could feel his interest.

"I believe we're individual consciousness using the body and mind as a means to become aware of the whole of itself through experience," I said.

We sat in silence for another ten minutes. I tucked his hand under the blanket and took in his sleeping face. He was pale and drawn. He was close.

Just as I was at the door, he opened his mouth and out came, "Possible."

I burst into a smile. Possible was a shift. Possible was an opening. *Possible* was a higher frequency.

The last piece of advice my father gave me before he died was, "Always have something to look forward to, Jocie." I have tried to honor that and the many other gifts he gave me.

The day came when the lawyer arrived to read my father's will. I remember hearing, "Under no circumstances is there to be a funeral or memorial of any kind."

"Fine," I said, almost immediately. "We'll have a dinner party."

We had dinner for a hundred in my father's honor. There was a run on martinis with the over-eighty set. We sang songs and told our stories. Samantha played the flute. My brother, who has an angelic voice but is too shy to sing in public, sang "Danny Boy." People cried, releasing their grief. People laughed, celebrating the wonder of life. Everyone agreed it was a beautiful day.

Alone outside, cleaning up the last of the party debris, I felt the wind pick up and blow through the chimes that hang in the magnolia tree. I took it as a sign of approval from my father. Henry loved a good dinner party.

Exercise: Always Have Something to Look Forward To

The advice to always have something to look forward to was one of my father's greatest gifts. I learned that when I was going through a particularly difficult time, like a medical recovery or pushing through a series of very unpleasant tasks, having something fun to look forward to made all the difference. It goes hand in hand with my dad's advice to Samantha about the importance of making memories. Plus, as Henry would tell you, when you create new memories, you always have a new story to tell!

Henry's lesson:

- Make a list of five things you'd *love* to do. For example:

    * Go see the Picasso exhibit at the museum.

    * Take some watercolors to the beach and paint.

    * Take a hike in the woods or mountains.

    * Go to the theatre.

    * Go to a special store, nursery, restaurant, friend's house, etc.

    * Chose three of these things and put them on your calendar for future fun. Honor these personal dates. Strive to say what you do and do what you say. Strive to always have something on the calendar you know you'll enjoy.

- Now, make a list of five places you'd like to travel.

  * Paris

  * New York

  * Italy

  * Vancouver Island

  * Scotland

- Choose one of these places and put it on your calendar in the future. It doesn't matter if it's a year or two ahead. Choose a date you can believe in.

  * Start a list of what you need to do to get there.

  * Study maps of the city.

  * Make a list of what you're going to do while visiting.

  * Continue developing the dream by checking out accommodations, events, places to visit, restaurants, etc.

  * Put money toward purchasing your ticket and accommodations. It doesn't matter if it's a dollar a week to start. Put something there every week.

  * Once you're ready, *buy the ticket!*

* When you find yourself in a blue mood, check your calendar and anticipate what's coming up for you.

Choosing which activities to put on the calendar is a simple exercise in manifestation—one that involves imagining, seeking joy, memory-making, and raising your vibration. What could be better?

Don't be stingy. Slather your calendar with things to look forward to—make Henry proud!

CHAPTER 12

Walking My Mother
Back Home

"Tell your friend that in his death, a part of you dies and goes with him. Wherever he goes, you also go. He will not be alone."

—J. KRISHNAMURTI

IN LATE OCTOBER 2016, I FLEW HOME FOR MY MOTHER'S NINETIETH birthday. We had just finished our usual four-day visit. *Usual* in the sense that for the first two days, I was sure things had changed between us. But by the third day, my mother would become punishingly hostile, leaving me to wonder what I'd done wrong. By the fourth day, her unexpressed resentment was so thick that I couldn't wait to get out of there.

I had come a long way in my life. I was well into my sixties and deeply grateful for all that I had learned and all I was blessed with. I had a loving relationship with my husband, who'd become my best friend. We'd raised a beautiful daughter, who was the light of my life. I'd learned to take my greatest challenges and turn them into my most valuable lessons. And with every spiritual awakening, I fashioned a key and passed it on to my students.

But try as I might, I couldn't seem to change the dynamic with my mother. It was the source of my greatest sadness and confusion in life. Over the years, I'd discovered four days with her was my limit. After that, I'd engage in the toxicity hook, line, and sinker, and I'd hate myself for it—compounding the fracture.

Making it to ninety years old is a big deal. Although my mother was tough as nails, I took note on the visit that she seemed particularly morose and uncharacteristically frail. I worried even more about her living alone. She was still working but battling her crew. She was battling a lot of things—it had become her way. She was worried that her lead man was stealing her clients. I reminded her that her plan was to leave him the business, and maybe it was time to step down. The suggestion outraged her. She insisted she had the same energy as twenty years earlier. She didn't. Her working days were over. She was in denial.

Denial

I tried to broach the subject of her living alone. Maybe it was time to think about more help? She had a four-bedroom house, and it would be easy to organize a space for someone else to live there, help her, and still give her privacy. The idea appalled her. She had been living alone for forty-two years, and she was *just fine*, thank you. She was in denial about this issue, too.

I took note. I knew it was time for a change, and I knew she would fight tooth and nail against anything that meant she didn't have full control over every aspect of her life.

She was in denial about pretty much everything: her age, her health, her needs, her happiness. In retrospect, I recognize this as the first stage in Elizabeth Kubler-Ross's theory of the five stages of grief regarding death and dying: denial, anger, bargaining, depression, and acceptance.

I decided to talk to my brother about the situation and the problem of living so far away at this time in her life. I knew change was in the wind, but the timing couldn't be worse, as I was facing my own existential crisis.

After our visit, I went into the city for some much-needed R & R. I'd been teaching for thirty years. I was bone-tired, and felt I'd missed the off-ramp somewhere. I was drained. It was clear I needed a new game, but I didn't have the foggiest idea what it might be.

My first night in Manhattan, I had one of those only in New York, close-down-the-restaurant dinners with a friend. I cried about my mother and laughed to release the pain. I couldn't believe that I was still struggling with mommy issues at my age. Needless to say, we got a bit tipsy. When I returned to my little Airbnb, I crashed.

The next morning, I checked my phone. There were fifteen messages! All of them said, "Your mother had a stroke last night."

I froze. A terrible feeling overwhelmed me. As I was enjoying a beautiful dinner, laughing with my friend in the city, my mother was having a stroke. She was going through seven circles of hell— and I was enjoying myself. I felt overwhelming guilt.

I threw on clothes and raced up to Montefiore Medical Center in the Bronx, where she had been sent for testing. Her speech was seriously impaired, and she was shaky on her feet. What little strength she had, she spent on rage—striking out at me and anyone around her. I understood. She was terrified and vulnerable. Her body had betrayed her, and worst of all, she'd lost control over her life.

I understood it well because I'd inherited this trait from her, like a contagion. When I lost control or felt vulnerable, particularly in a hospital, I'd strike out like a cornered animal to protect myself. Although mindfulness had made me aware of how nasty I would get when distrustful, I couldn't let it go any more than she could. The best I could do was say it out loud: "I know I'm being a bitch, and I'm so sorry, but I can't quite let it go!"

It took me four days to get her out of there and into the Helen Hayes Rehab Center. She was granted a three-week stay at what many consider to be the best rehab center on the East Coast, but she spent the entire time angling to get out. She knew her days were numbered, and she wanted to spend every minute she had in her beloved home.

Once I knew she was in good hands at Helen Hayes, I went back to Snedens and called my brother. I clearly needed help. I needed to return home to California immediately and arrange my life so I could be on call for her. I needed to put my acting studio on hiatus and attend to a medical procedure of my own. I was hoping my brother, who also lives in California, could fly in to receive our mother when she got out of rehab. Maybe he could stay a couple of weeks, and then I'd come and take over.

I told my brother it was time to address the fact that she needed help but didn't want it any more than she had *before* the stroke. It was a tough request because my brother has a child with special needs at home, and I knew his absence would be particularly hard on his beautiful wife, Roxanna. But he said yes on a dime. The plan was for the two of us to ping-pong back and forth while we figured out a long-term plan for our mother's care.

As per hospital instructions, my mother could no longer be home alone. It was obvious she needed care, but she had burned through any number of assistants with her misplaced rage. Now, she was calling people up and scheming to get out of rehab before my brother's arrival. It was hard enough to understand her in the room—on the phone, it was impossible.

Anger

The night before my brother flew in to pick her up, I got a call from one of her neighbors. It seemed the town planned to re-tar the road in front of my mother's house *that day*! There was no traffic allowed in or out, and my mother would have to wait another twenty-four hours for the tar to dry.

Although she had just received her release papers, the people at Helen Hayes said that under the circumstances, she could stay an extra night. They were as unhappy as she was. My mother had become verbally abusive to everyone there.

Meanwhile, Mom was having none of it! She convinced her last loyal friend to bust her out of Helen Hayes and drop her off as close to the house as possible. From there, she walked through the sticky tar with the assistance of her cane, and when she got to her house at the bottom of the hill, she threw away her shoes. My brother did the same when he arrived several hours later. They were home.

What made the trek even more astounding was that my mother was legally blind. Misdiagnosed macular degeneration had taken her sight some twenty years earlier. Although she could see a little light in her periphery and knew the lay of the land in Snedens, the walk down the hill was an exercise in trust, or foolishness—or both.

My mother had gotten the thing she wanted most. Unfortunately, her solution was to annihilate anyone in her vicinity to assure victory. It was a war waged over control. I knew the shame of it. Such behavior not only makes it difficult for others to like you but also makes it impossible to like yourself, which is dangerous to human health on every level.

My brother stayed for a couple of weeks, and we discussed by phone how to proceed. We wanted to honor her wishes for independence as much as we could, but the stroke made it clear they were unrealistic. In the end, we cobbled together a calendar where someone would be working with her, stopping by, handling errands, or checking in every day—usually twice a day. Most importantly, we had people who would call us if needed. But for now, we could take a breath and think about what to do next.

My mother was a bundle of resentment about the situation, and her unexpressed rage had a new target: my brother and me. I understood why she was so bitter and mean. She couldn't bear being dependent, and she wasn't going to let go of her freedom without a fight. This stage of life can be brutal. I saw it with my father as well. On reflection, I saw her wrath as stage two of the five stages of grief—anger.

Anger about your life coming to an end seems fair enough, but my people are not very good at anger. We either strap it in until it turns into cancer or lash out savagely—then poison ourselves with guilt.

After my brother settled my mother into her new schedule, he flew back home. It was two weeks before Christmas. I was to fly in and take his place, but my mother's only Christmas wish was to be left alone. She told us she'd do all the rehab steps and keep to the schedule on the calendar *if* we would just leave her alone. She'd finally gotten rid of us, and she *didn't* want us back.

She insisted I cancel my trip. So, after checking in with her team, my brother and I decided to give her what she was angling for—space from her children. We keep close tabs on her by phone. Although I didn't see it at the time, we were at the third stage—bargaining.

Bargaining

For the next two months, my mother rallied. She worked with a speech therapist, and her voice got stronger. She walked around the house and climbed the stairs several times a day for exercise. She was anxious to get back to work and wrote long lists on her clipboards. She even seemed to enjoy having people around to help her.

She was bargaining: if I do *this*, can I have my life back again?

Depression

But when friends stopped phoning because they couldn't understand her, and neighbors stopped dropping by because it was too sad to see her so compromised, she found herself profoundly depressed. Without being able to work, the fight in her was gone. Without the high of creating, she just gave up.

Stage four—depression.

Acceptance

On February 18, 2017, just three months after the stroke, the phone rang in the middle of the night. I heard my mother's voice on the other end of the line. "Come home, Jocie," she said. "I'm dying."

I called the airlines, booked a flight out of LAX, and pulled out "Big Red"—the largest suitcase I own. As I piled in clothes, I tried to deep-breathe my way through the onslaught of adrenaline. I wanted to move forward consciously. I wanted to rise to the occasion. I wanted to be there for her at my best, without succumbing to all the buttons I knew were about to be pushed.

I left for LAX at sunrise. Pink clouds bounced off the Santa Monica mountains. It was a perfect sixty-eight degrees. I looked back at our house, and my winter garden and silently said my goodbyes. I had no idea how long I'd be gone.

In my heart, I have two homes. California has been my home for over forty years. It represents the life I've created with my husband, Miles, and our daughter, Samantha. We'd bought our current 1938 Cape Cod house, nine blocks from the ocean, together with Henry when it became clear he could no longer safely live alone. For the last seven years of my father's life, we were three generations under one roof. He's been gone for eighteen years now.

But my mother's house in the country, the house I grew up in, would always resonate as my *home* home. Home of my childhood. Home where I first located my soul.

The flight took forever, I had a layover in Atlanta, and my bag was the last off the carousel at JFK. The house in Snedens is thirty minutes up the Palisades Parkway on the Jersey side of the George Washington Bridge. But it's an hour-and-a-half trek from the airport in traffic.

As I got into a hired car for the ride out to Snedens, it started to snow. It had been snowing on and off for days, and now it was coming down fast. We crawled along the FDR Drive in a bubble of white, the views of the river completely obscured. I practiced breathing as the miles clicked by.

Finally, we were on the George Washington Bridge—ah, the last leg home. I arrived at the house around 9:30 that night. The snow had slowed by the time we got there, but there was a good foot and a half on the ground. Snow's good for the soul, I thought—mine anyway. Like a baptism, I lifted my face to it—silently crying out to be blessed.

As I stood in the giant kitchen garden with my enormous suitcase—ankles sunk in the snow, face lifted to the sky—I tried to summon the compassion and forgiveness I'd need to comfort my mother, whose love I still longed for and knew I'd never receive. Somehow, I had to let all that go. It was time to love her unconditionally, even though she'd do her best to make that difficult.

Someone had turned on the outside light to welcome me, but inside the house was completely dark. The last time I was home, my mother had taken to keeping *all* the lights on, *all* the time. She wanted to soak up every bit of light she could. Seeing the house dark made me realize she'd given up on her eyes completely. There was smoke coming from the chimney, and I wondered who'd made the fire. I banged open the Dutch door to the kitchen.

"Hello?" I yelled out, slamming Big Red on the ancient wooden floor. I didn't know what to expect. Was she back in the bedroom? Gone to the hospital? With someone?

"In here," she summoned. "Sorry! Sorry darling," she said, as she turned on one light after another, making her way to the kitchen with ease.

She knew every inch of her house and glided through it effortlessly. She was so good at handling her sight impairment that you would forget how bad it was unless you left something somewhere it didn't belong, and she stumbled over it.

"BALLS! Who left this here?!" she'd howl.

That was her big, bad curse word: "balls." She was the only person I've ever heard use that expression. She only used it when she was red hot mad—but it always made me laugh out loud.

"Hello, darling. Thank you for coming," she garbled as we kissed hello. I could understand her, but just barely.

Having been with my godmother at the time of her death and my father at the time of his, I knew immediately my mother wasn't dying. But she was done. She was ninety years old, blind, tired, and unable to be understood.

Living with Dying

Since her stroke, we had talked on the phone often, but I'd always initiated the call. She seemed to appreciate my desire to understand her, but asking me for help was not in her vocabulary.

And yet she had called…

As I sat by the fire in the same wingback chair I'd curled up in since I was a child, I watched as she tried to form the words as best she could. She talked, and talked, and didn't stop talking for a good long while. It was easy to see she was hungry for conversation and needed someone to listen. I encouraged her stories and worked on understanding her. I did my best, even if I sometimes had to pretend.

She was beautiful—always had been, with her steel-blue eyes that didn't work anymore, her Greta Garbo haircut, and the highest cheekbones known to man. I took her in, wondering what it must be like for her.

After fourteen years of marriage, my stepfather had left my mother for wife number three—what goes around comes around, I guess. Now he was on wife number four, a woman just a *tad* older than his daughters. After their divorce, my mother came into her own. It was the first time she'd been without a man, and she was forced to grow up through the trauma of abandonment in order to survive.

Now, she felt abandoned again, "put out to pasture" by her friends—but truth be told, she had little tolerance for people her own age, and her relentless criticism of others tore away at any loyalty they may have felt for her. I thought of gently pointing this out but realized the time had passed. What she needed now was to vent.

After her long monologue and a few glasses of wine, I broached the subject. "Hey, Mom?"

"Hmmm?" she answered.

"I need to talk to you about something," I said.

"Hmmm?" again.

"Well...you know you're a very strong woman. I mean, you're a survivor—you've often said those exact words to me: 'I'm a survivor.'"

She answered with a nod.

"Well, you know your body takes orders from that strength. I mean, you overcame the one-kidney deal."

She nodded again; talking about her health always got her attention.

"And, you know…your heart," I said.

"Angina…Princewater," she interjected.

"Prinz*metal*," I answered, unsure why I felt compelled to correct her. What did it matter at this point? What did it matter at all?

"Very, very rare," she shot back, wearing her illness like a badge of honor.

"Right," I said. "So, the fact that you're able, at your age, Mom—I mean you climbed the stairs, you took a bath, you got dressed and combed your hair, you wrapped yourself in your Hermès shawl and put food out on the counter for me. And…did you make the fire?"

"Marjorie started it this morning. I just feed it wood," she snapped, as if guilty of an indiscretion. A blind woman stoking a fire. What's wrong with this picture?

"But Mom…" I started again, "You opened a bottle of wine—"

"But it was *hard*, Jocie! It's all too hard. I don't want to live like this anymore."

"Mom, I understand you *want* to die—"

"I'M DONE!" she exploded.

"I get it!" I said. "But can't you see…this is not what a dying person looks like."

There was a long pause. My mother was all about how things *looked*. She hadn't thought about death from her favorite angle.

"What does it look like then?" she asked, sounding like a child.

"Well, for one thing, you'd be in bed," I said.

My mother lost it. "I CAN'T JUST LIE AROUND IN THE BED ALL DAY LONG!"

I said it as gently as possible. "That's because you're not dying, Mommy."

What else could I say?

I didn't go back to California. My mother asked me to call hospice the next day. She climbed into her four-poster bed—the bed she would no longer make every morning at 6 a.m., the bed that had survived two divorces—and she assumed the position of dying.

She stopped eating and measured her water intake. She was defiant. If anyone even hinted at the idea that she shouldn't—or couldn't— orchestrate her own death, they were eviscerated. It was the ultimate control. She was determined to depart life as she had lived it—on her own terms. She was impossibly mean and wonderfully admirable all at the same time.

With every nastiness she flung at me, I practiced not *listing*—you know, that long list we keep adding to, the proof that "you done me wrong"—I prayed for us to move past our issues before she was gone. I prayed for the compassion to love her unconditionally. When I failed and the tears overwhelmed me, I went out and talked to the trees. My trees. My loves. My stability.

She gave orders—LOTS of orders. She loved clipboards and took to writing her thoughts down more than she'd speak. I think it must have been a shock to hear her own voice. Inside her head, she heard the words perfectly—but the sounds that came out of her mouth were a betrayal of the tongue. Even the acute hearing she'd developed since losing her sight was now failing. One day she wrote, "No see, no speak, no hear—no fun."

God, I felt for her.

What made her happy was control. What made her happy was controlling me. Controlling me meant that I never got it right. How could I? I wasn't her. I swear if she could have climbed into my body and taken it over, she would have.

It was the ultimate test for me, and I was fraying under her attacks. Some of the aides told me I should go home, that she was saying horrible things behind my back. One even said she was out to kill me. But I knew her paranoia was from not eating. My mother flexed her strength best against an enemy; even an invented one would do. Who better to play the role than me? She knew I'd never leave her. How could I? She was a broken child who needed me, *and* she was my mother.

We had a team at this point. There was a cherished housekeeper, Elsa, who'd been with my mother for twenty-some years. There was a secretary of sorts, who tended toward drama and often told me things I didn't need or want to hear. There was a dear friend and neighbor who served as a trusted executive assistant, for lack of a better term. There was Nurse Nancy, whom the state paid to come in once a week. She'd been keeping track of my mother's health for many years and was a valuable advisor. There were hospice visits. And for her last five or six weeks, there was a team of three Jamaican caregivers—angel-women who bathed her, changed her, and knew the stages of death intimately. They were kind, caring, and unafraid. They were a God-given blessing.

Among us, we endeavored to keep a calm space in the madness and drama death tends to write for itself.

People wrote notes and dropped by to visit. She would weigh in on her feelings—forgive them or reject them. Then, depending on the effect she wanted to create, she would deign to see them—or not. They would wait outside the kitchen, top of the Dutch door open as I checked in with her. There were people it pained me to turn away.

"I'm so sorry. She's sleeping," I would say. A number of people felt I was blocking them from a visit. I was just following orders. It was her show, her last chapter, and I felt she got to write it exactly as she wanted, even if I was often cast as the villain. It wasn't personal; it was just death and dying.

There were a few beautiful letters from faraway friends, a generation who knew the magic of letter writing. These were kept in a special drawer, tied up with a ribbon, and I would take them out and read them to her when she asked.

"Read Júlio's letter again, please." That particular letter had half a dozen reads—it was love in an envelope. In the end, she reconnected to most of her tribe, but not all.

There were some "important" friends who neither wrote, nor called, nor came to visit. There were dear friends who considered themselves "family" who might have flown in but waited for the memorial. There were cherished friends close by who chose to stay alienated.

"Everyone deals with death in their own way," I explained when she'd ask about these people, hurt and confused. "Everyone gets a pass on death. It's one of death's graces."

After a while, my mother and I began to form a bond that seemed oddly effortless and natural. She had brought me into the world, and I felt privileged to see her out. It occurred to me that walking someone home is the most intimate thing we do. That being born and dying are the biggest events in our life, and it's an honor to be present at either.

As the fight in her subsided, her light intensified until the day came when I could *feel* her love for me—our hearts connected where the words could not. One evening, after kissing her good night, I went outside, sat under Tree, and sobbed. *My god!* I thought. *We were meant to be best friends! We just somehow missed the off-ramp for that particular adventure.*

Through the sadness of it all, I was grateful. Grateful that I was there with her. Grateful that she was my mother and that I'd learned the many lessons I had from knowing her.

And grateful that our hearts had found each other once again.

Gratitude

Gratitude comes not from the head but the heart. It is a euphoric feeling of thankfulness for the large and small miracles in life.

I believe reflecting on our blessings is the single most powerful prayer there is. To be grateful is to reinforce everything that's right in the world. From saying grace over a meal to our final prayers at night—acknowledging our blessings is the most effective step we can take in recognizing and cultivating more joy in our lives.

Gratitude and acknowledgment are also important business practices. I tell my students when they take a meeting, get advice, or receive help: it's not only polite but also *feels* good to express your appreciation with some kind of response.

Your time is the most precious commodity you have—so is theirs! A heartfelt letter or a small gift is appropriate. And it's fun!

If you book a job, send the casting director flowers and thank them for thinking of you—you can afford to now. If you don't book the job, send them a *short* note and thank them for calling you in. You are cultivating a relationship.

If you take a long meeting with someone who advises you, send a small gift and a personal note to thank them for their time and attention. If you're short on money, *make* a card, tie a balloon on the door, leave a perfect peach in the mailbox—but give a little something of yourself back. It doesn't matter what the gesture is, as long as it's from your heart.

Remember this: when someone goes out of their way to give you their time, and you *don't* acknowledge it, it's an incomplete communication. A special, hand-picked little gift is how you earn your right to take the advice they offered.

As you get to know people, listen for what they're interested in. Collect things on your travels that catch your attention, and have them on hand to give as gifts. Keep a basket of cards to inspire handwritten notes.

I've had more than one person pick up on the fact that I love the garden. I had a student once who brought me a small, potted peace rose. It knocked me out! I felt like she went out of her way on my behalf. That little plant went into a bigger pot and became a bigger plant. Finally, it went into the garden, where it flourishes to this day. Every time I see it bloom, I think of that person—magic.

We do well when we practice the art of goodwill. Be generous in your expressions of gratitude and you will not only make *yourself* feel better about this journey you are on but also inspire generosity in others—something we need more of in this day and age.

Bonus Exercise:
Practice Gratitude

When I talk about gratitude, I tell my actors it's a capacity—one that, like *you*, is either expanding or contracting.

I recommend spending ten minutes a day reflecting on your blessings. This small practice will expand your capacity for gratitude and enhance your level of enthusiasm beyond measure.

Here are some other ways you can practice gratitude, thereby elevating the quality of your life.

- The art of letter writing

    * Keep an ongoing list of people who have contrib-
      uted to your life in some way. It could include your

second-grade teacher, a hairdresser who gave you sage advice, or even Stephen King—thanking him for a book you enjoyed.

* Pick someone on your list, and send them a *hand-written* letter thanking them for their positive influence. It can be short—one sentence even. Think of how wonderful you feel when you go through the monthly bills and find a personal letter from someone. This intimate act of goodwill has become a rare gift in this day and age. Write a letter at least once a week. This simple act of magic-making will open up the flows of communication in your life in unimaginable ways!

- The perfect gift

* Take yourself on a little shopping spree. Pick up some cards or beautiful paper to make your own cards. Look for some small gifts to start a gift-giving stash. Pick someone on your list, and send them a little something.

* If you're short on money, take a walk on the beach or in your local woods. A shell or stone that speaks to you makes a lovely present.

* Be aware that you are taking something from a sacred space. Give thanks for drawing your attention to the gift. Ask permission to take it. This exercise in respect will expand your capacity for reverence—something we could always use more of.

You are learning to communicate in new ways.
You are cultivating synchronicity, and the under-
lying mysticism life has to offer.

- Gratitude for others

  * Make a practice of telling your spouse, partner,
    friend, or even a complete stranger something
    you enjoy about them every day.

- Gratitude for the planet

  * The next time you notice a beautiful bird, or a
    stream of sunlight in the late afternoon, or the
    wind moving through the leaves of a tree as if
    to say hello—or any of the seemingly random
    moments that complement each day—take
    a moment to give thanks. Chances are that
    beautiful gesture, in that singular moment,
    was experienced by you and you alone.

White Tulips

One day, the notes and visitors stopped coming altogether, and
my mother commented on it.

I could see the hurt on her face and decided a little magic was
in order. I went out and bought two dozen white tulips and
wrote a note that said, "You are loved, Judy Tomkins." I left
no signature.

"Mom, someone left these outside the kitchen door!" I told her, as I brought in the flowers.

My mother lit up like a Christmas tree! "What? What is it?" she asked, her arms fully extended like a child reaching for a present—so tiny and thin.

I described the tulips as I placed them in her arms. The fact that there were two dozen was impressive. "What does the card say?"

I read the card. "'You are loved, Judy Tomkins.' No signature—Mom, they're from a secret admirer."

My mother swooned. "Misha!" she said. "Oh, my god! They're from Misha!"

I felt like I had done a very good thing and a very bad thing all at the same time. "Well, Mom—you can't assume they're from anybody. There's no signature, honey."

"I know," she said with certainty. "I know they're from him."

What followed became more and more bizarre. First, there were her orders on where the tulips should go and how they should be displayed.

"Put five in the black vase on the fireplace mantle," she said. "Maybe some could go in the window, some on the nightstand... and...can you get them over my head?" she asked, as she waved her hand in an imperious arch over the crown of her head.

The Jamaican angel and I looked at each other.

At this point in time, my mother had chosen to wear a black silk sleeping mask to protect her eyes from the light. The sight of her, tiny-thin in the middle of her four-poster bed, propped up in her long white nightie, surrounded by white linens, with her Greta Garbo haircut, those cheekbones, and her black silk sleeping mask—add to the image two dozen white tulips floating over her head—well, life and art had become indistinguishable. I could *see* the painting she had in her mind. I even knew the artist she would have paint it.

Once the tulips were in place, awaiting a visitor who never came, I wondered whether it was good magic or bad. On the one hand, she took the opportunity to convince herself that the person she wanted to say goodbye to most in life had sent her two dozen white tulips. On the other, she had obsessed over him for days, bringing back all the pain of whatever happened that kept her cherished friend away.

At some point, my mother began to sleep and dream in a new way. It wasn't long before sleeping and dreaming became her favorite thing. She wouldn't want to do the things laid out for the day. She wouldn't want to see anyone. She'd urgently tell us she had to go back to sleep.

"It's important," she'd say. She wanted to float out on a dream— who could blame her?

One night, she dreamed she died. For the whole next day, she told us, "I died last night. I heard it on the radio."

She was terribly disappointed to find she was still here.

The day came when I kissed her good morning, and she was unresponsive. Her Jamaican angel said, "Don't bother her now; she's traveling."

Just before she left us to take those final steps alone, she ordered us to "listen to the new guy—he knows what he's talking about."

I assumed she had accepted the guide who had come for her. She never regained consciousness.

In the end, it had taken three months. She went to bed, stopped eating, raged, calmed, and slipped away in the night. She used her will of steel to control her own death. She was a force. I did my best to support her.

Doing the Best We Can

My mother was an artist. Before she lost her eyesight, she had been a photographer. She had proudly published two books of photographs and enjoyed several shows at the Leo Castelli Gallery, home to the work of Jasper Johns and Bob Rauschenberg, among other titans of the time.

She was also a landscape architect, creating beautiful perennial gardens and park-like grounds. Her work had a "wild feel" about it—that was her signature. She wanted her designs to *belong* to the place. In spite of her blindness, she continued to design until her stroke. She didn't need her eyes in the garden; she could *imagine* what she wanted and had a loyal crew to execute her vision.

When she was taking pictures or designing gardens, my mother was the best of herself. She was like another person, confident and generous. She was a perfect example of an artist bouncing from the highest frequencies of inspiration to the lowest vibration of narcissism and self-loathing. The whiplash could be hard to take. But she was an artist through and through, and when she lost hope of ever creating again, there wasn't anything more to live for.

My mother had been abandoned as a child. She was born just before the Great Depression, and to make matters worse, my grandmother was disowned by *her* mother for having a child with an artist fourteen years her senior. I'm not sure which was worse—the age difference or that my grandfather was an artist. When they couldn't afford her, my grandparents would farm my mother out. They'd leave her with other people, tell her they'd be back for Christmas, and not show up for a year or more. It was brutal. My mother never forgave her parents. Abandonment was at the root of my mother's every issue. It permeated her life like a virus in her DNA.

Although my mother and I had a difficult relationship, she taught me a great deal about the art of living. I attribute my joy in keeping an aesthetic home, tending a garden, and cooking to her. She gave her love freely to these things because they wouldn't—in fact *couldn't*—betray her. Her life in art is where her beauty resided, and God knows, she was a beauty.

I have found that habits of respect and compassion are easily learned by example, but if you come to these qualities by choice, they must be ardently practiced. To practice anything effectively, you must be awake and in the moment. Slip out of the moment, and I can become the best of bitches!

I am actively *practicing* kindness and compassion. Of course, I fall back on bad habits and fail miserably at times, and I'm horribly mean to myself when I do. As if being hard on ourselves helps anyone. I suppose I think if I'm hard on myself, I'll *try* harder. What a fallacy! As I tell my students, "trying" and a dime won't get you a cup of coffee. The definition of try is *to make an attempt or effort*. Nothing about getting the job done.

Self-denigration is a waste of time. It's just *stalling*—it keeps us from changing into who we'd like to be. The answer to change is simpler: recognize, let go, and move on. That's the practice.

The greatest lesson of all may be forgiveness. Forgiving self. Forgiving others. Recognizing that we are all doing the best we can and that we are exactly where we need to be to learn our next lesson. Sometimes we get it. Sometimes it takes a lifetime or two.

I had no idea what the landscape of my mother's death might look like, but I knew the end of her life was at hand. I knew I wanted to fulfill her wishes. I knew I wanted her to be as comfortable as possible—physically, mentally, and emotionally. I knew I wanted to show up for her as my best self. Most importantly, I wanted her to feel loved.

I had no idea how long it would take, how all-consuming it would be, or how hopelessly lost I'd feel at times. I had no idea how helpful people would be—or how hurtful. There were places my mother and I traveled together in that final journey I'd never imagined. There were things that happened along the way that seemed unfathomable.

I meditated every day, often more than once. I observed her without judgment. I practiced mindfulness in the moment as best as I could. I brought the beauty and spirit of nature into her room daily. Every morning, I showed up with the intention to move forward, one foot in front of the other, as my best self.

And I *knew* the destination. I couldn't *see* it—but it was inevitable.

Did I fail at times? Yes. Were there moments that shocked me? Yes. Did we reach our destination feeling we had exhausted every avenue to get there? Yes. Was there beauty as well as ugliness? Yes. Did I grow in the process? More than I imagined possible.

I wanted something from my mother that she didn't have to give. At my worst, I blamed her for it. At my *very* worst, I punished her by withholding the love she needed. Talk about the Law of Attraction—*I withhold love from you and wonder why you don't love me?*

It's our job as children to do a little better than the previous generation. We learn by observation. We learn from the good and emulate it. We learn from the bad and do our best to improve it. Hopefully, we're evolving. My mother did a little better than hers. I've done a bit better than mine. My daughter will do better than me—and so it goes.

I am grateful to have been there for both my parents when their time came to say goodbye. Grateful for all the many gifts they gave me. Grateful for the love we shared and for their part in shaping me into the person I've become.

The endgame between parents and children is one of the most challenging things we do; at least, it was for me. We're not educated when it comes to death. When it comes to death, we all just do the best we can.

Exercise:
Love Expressed Is Love Manifest

I want to give you an exercise to help you connect with the people you love and remind you to actively express that love while you're able.

Close your eyes, and listen to your breath.

Inhale deeply: I breathe in ease.

Exhale slowly: I breathe out tension.

Repeat for ten minutes. If thoughts come up, simply note "thinking" and focus your attention back on your breath.

After ten minutes, open your eyes. When you are ready, open your journal and breathe into your heart.

- List three things you love. For example:

    * I love my husband, MILES.

    * I love GARDENS.

    * I love **ARTISTS**.

- List two ways to express each of those three loves. For example:

    * MILES:

- * Make a special dinner that includes his favorite foods.

  * Surprise him by sewing those two missing buttons on his favorite jacket.

- GARDENS:

  * Order tulips to be planted in the fall.

  * Cut roses for the dining table.

- ARTISTS

  * Donate to a non-profit organization that supports art in schools.

  * Write a love letter to artists that might encourage and uplift them—like a book, perhaps?

- Finish the job by executing your ideas.

Birth and death are like the front and back cover to our existence here on Earth. Although we are born to every corner of the world and in every condition imaginable, we have overlooked and disregarded this physical plane upon which we have been granted life.

We have brought Mother Earth to her knees. I believe if we are to evolve at all, we must wake up to the beauty of our home, this Eden of a planet, and listen to and care for our mother, nature.

As for the *only* inevitable event in our lives—death—it would seem that since the last moment of every story is always the same, it's the pages that come between that are important. And these pages of our life's story either flip by unattended or are written with a fierce desire to make the best of this gift of time we have here on our beautiful planet.

Conclusion

"The purpose of our lives is to add value to the people of this generation and those that follow. Nature is a totally efficient, self-regenerating system. If we discover the laws that govern this system and live synergistically within them, sustainability will follow and humankind will be a success."

—R. BUCKMINSTER FULLER

AFTER MY MOTHER'S DEATH, THERE WAS THE FAMILY HOME TO PUT IN order. I needed to declutter, deep clean, open all the windows, and breathe fresh air into the place. I needed to pull the house together for my mother's memorial and, ultimately, for sale.

My brother, David, came for a month to help prepare for the memorial. We scrubbed and organized all day, and when the sun went down, we'd enjoy supper on the terrace—chatting about memories, drinking wine, and gazing at fireflies. Often, we'd just sit in stillness, taking in the summer night—the bugs, the breezes, the reflection of the moon on the water. Our mother had died, and we were closing a profound chapter in our lives. You have to be very close to someone to sit in silence for long periods of time—it's an intimate thing to me. It feels healthy, like a delicate balance—like peace.

There's never been air-conditioning in my mother's house, and there were some *dog* days that summer, but we soldiered through. We'd work and sweat all day and shower or swim at night—stealing dips in the neighbor's pools, who were away at their summer homes, just as we'd done as children. After we cooled down, we'd have gin and tonics and cigarettes, like the grown-ups used to. I smoked that summer—dumb, I know—but I enjoyed every cigarette. It was somehow poetic. David had given me my first puff when I was twelve. Smoking and swimming were part of our common bond. Now here we were in our sixties, feeling sixteen as we said goodbye to our childhood home forever.

We held my mother's memorial about two months after her death at the little white church that rang the bell on Sunday mornings. We never attended worship there, except once in a blue moon, when we'd go on Christmas Eve. After a short service, everyone walked down to a neighbor's waterfront estate to celebrate my mother's life.

It was a beautiful day in July. My mother had designed the property, including a magical stretch of woodland at one end—a perfect spot for walking meditations. The gardens were at their summer height. This particular property was her most beautiful accomplishment, and that day, the place was in its glory.

People flew in from other states or drove out from the city. Friends arrived from New England, and neighbors walked down the hill to gather in her honor. I could *feel* her there, among the hundred or so people—floating about in the breezes, saying her farewells.

The day after the memorial, my brother and his family flew back to Los Angeles.

When my husband and I were finally alone, he held me in his arms, in my childhood room. As I released the stored-up tears, he whispered, "Well done, Jocie. Well done."

It was as if his love reached all the way back to those lonely days of my youth, healing that time and place. He seemed to be stroking my seven-year-old head, saying, "It's all right; I'm here now."

We had two days alone in the house as a family—Miles, our daughter, Samantha, and her new fiancé, Matthew. Being alone with them was like a dream. I felt deeply blessed.

And then, they too had to go.

I was alone again, with a new task at hand. I had to sell the house. I had to let go of that piece of my heart. It seemed like I didn't know anything. I didn't know how long it would take to sell. I didn't know how long it would take to empty. I didn't know if or when I would return to teaching. I didn't know...I didn't know...I didn't know. I'm a person who *likes* to know. I'm a person who likes order. I've been called a control freak by more than one.

The thing about *not* knowing is you have to trust. And when you ask for help and *know* that you'll receive it, your guides show up. Never is that communion more alive than when you *ask* for help, trust it to arrive, acknowledge it when it does—and give thanks.

Too often, I forget to ask.

During the process of selling the house, I developed an itch of sorts. For some unknown reason, I had this growing desire to have a pied-à-terre in the city. *Pied-à-terre* is a French word meaning "foot on earth." For some reason, I wanted a foot in New York City—the city of my first independent steps, the city of endless possibility.

It seemed like a ridiculously extravagant dream. I couldn't tell you *why* I wanted it or what I intended to do there. I certainly didn't need it. There was no compelling reason to justify the impulse. But there it was, this whisper. And this one desire felt like the only thing I had any certainty about.

As a teacher, I trained artists to follow that kind of impulse blindly. *Trust your impulses, and they will lead to something wonderful, even if unseen right now. Trust your instincts, and the reasons for them will eventually be revealed. Leap, and the net will appear.* But still…

My husband, a director who also teaches filmmaking at his alma mater, USC, is a firm believer in this quality of impulse. But still…

"It couldn't hurt to look—right?" he said, in an effort to encourage me. So, I started scouting around for a tiny place in the city to lease. The apartment literally dropped into my lap. My husband and I took it as a sign and leased the little studio on the Upper West Side, half a block from Central Park. I bought a loveseat and a reading chair and furnished the rest of the place with antiques, pottery, books, and art from Snedens. My mother's house provided everything, right down to a well-stocked kitchen, bar, band-aids, and a tool kit. The studio was an embrace—a sanctuary.

The house sold in under two months. Everyone was astonished by the speed. When the right buyer came along—the one who loved the house exactly the way it was—he offered full asking price. I gratefully accepted and thanked my "lucky stars" for sending him. I knew I'd had help from above.

Finally, the day came to say goodbye. Leaving the property was harder than leaving the house. It was almost a year to the day since my mother had suffered the stroke. It felt like three.

I stood on the hillside, looking out across the river, and breathed the place in. The wind arrived as if I'd summoned her. Suddenly, a million leaves swirled together, sounding like the rustling of petticoats past. As the autumn leaves rained down on me, I drank in their song.

I remember the sounds of the keys as I set them on the cold, black cement counter my mother so proudly designed. I left a note for the new owner with a glass of flowers from the autumn garden. I closed the Dutch door for the last time—and locked it for the first time ever. I popped the second set of keys in the mailbox across the street, and my friend Marjorie drove me to the new apartment in the city.

Once I was alone, I collapsed. I asked my family to give me a few weeks alone to do nothing. It was over. I needed to find my ground again. I cried from a depth I couldn't fathom. I kept hoping I was done, and then I'd go on another jag. I slept around the clock, woke up, and cried some more. I was grieving the loss of my life as I knew it. My mother was gone. My acting studio and twenty-five years of teaching—gone. The house in Snedens—gone. It felt like the Earth had been ripped from underneath me, and I was in freefall, wondering when I'd touch ground again.

I thought about death a lot, counted up my remaining years, and worried about how I'd spend them. I wandered aimlessly in the park, wondering what would become of me. I knew only one thing: I needed to let the tears flow freely until there were no more. I needed to let it all go so something new could come in.

Being surrounded by the beauty of my childhood made the apartment a refuge. One wall of the place has a fourteen-foot window with a magnificent tree right outside. She is so close; I can almost touch her. Framed by the window, she is more beautiful than any painting. I would take her in for hours, watching as, one by one, the breeze pulled the colored leaves off her limbs and dropped them like a thousand fallen gloves. It struck me that I'd never taken the time to witness that moment of emancipation before. Plucked from their mother by the wind, they swirled about like tiny kites. Untethered. Suddenly independent and alone. Free to enjoy their flight. They'd been born, grown through the season with their mother, briefly celebrated liberation—and now, filled to their maximum with nutrients, they peppered the Earth—offering the rest and best to the next generation.

Rebirth

We all have turning points brought about by the major events in our lives. Sometimes, we pass through quickly. Sometimes, it feels like an existential crisis—like we have to give up who we *think* we are without having any idea of who we're becoming. At best, we feel we are shedding some kind of skin and transforming into something different. We are. At worst, we feel like we're adrift at sea and will never touch land again.

During these times, we are living in a kind of purgatory—we are *between* who we were and who we are becoming.

After a few weeks, the tears slowed, and I forced myself to meditate again. I was shocked that within days, I could take in the beauty of the crisp fall air. Meditating helped me separate a little from my profound sense of loss. It gave me a break from the worry that my life was somehow over.

The tiny apartment in New York became my rebirth. A place to help me wake up to the next chapter in my life. A place to write and imagine and walk in the park. A place to check in with my *alone self.*

During that time in solitary, I listened to records from my childhood, read books, and tried to write. Not much came in the *in-between,* but it helped me to journal—so I scribbled around a bit. I saw friends and went to the theatre. I found a yoga studio and went to an energy clearing.

It was time for the question. I asked myself, *Jocie, if you could have anything in the world, barring all obstacles, what would it be?* Here's what came up:

- I wanted another chapter in my life.

- I wanted to pursue my own art in a way I hadn't before.

- I wanted to write.

It wasn't a lot, but it was something. It gave me hope. It gave me a new direction.

I had weathered the storm. I was resurrecting, reincarnating, breaking through to the other side. And I was stronger for it. My time in the *in-between* had taught me the power of embracing discomfort:

- I'd learned that it's okay to be uncomfortable. It's part of living.

- I'd learned to breathe into the unknown and trust that *whatever is happening right now is exactly as it should be.*

- I'd learned to breathe into the NOW—no matter the discomfort—and accept *what is*.

Accepting *what is* forms the bridge to what is becoming.

Bonus Exercise:
What to Do in the In-Between

Close your eyes, and listen to your breath for ten minutes.

Inhale: I breathe in trust.

Exhale: I breathe out fear.

When you find yourself in the *in-between*, that purgatory before rebirth:

- Acknowledge the *in-between* period as a time to process. Processing is about transcending difficulty, healing, and sometimes even shedding a skin. We are seeking our next evolution. Trust that change is inevitable, and you'll come through stronger.

- Ask yourself what you need to accept the experience. *If this discomfort goes on for a while, what might help me weather it better?* Is it breathing exercises? More meditation, walking, yoga, therapy, reading, writing, dancing, singing in a choir?

- Even when we're lost and lonely, we can experience gratitude for the summer breeze, the leaves turning color, fresh tracks in the snow, or the miraculous rebirth of spring. Loving life even when we're lost is the road to finding ourselves again.

- Take a look at your joy list and do those things.

- Accept the discomfort as part of positive change— rather than resisting it as something *wrong*. Breathe into it.

- We all have angels, guides, and a higher conscious-ness walking beside us. The *in-between* is a good time to trust and lean into them. Ask them for help, and acknowledge them when you receive it. Get famil-iar with this two-way communication of another kind.

- We have many lives in one lifetime. Draw a sketch or a map of your incarnations this time around. Start by moving through your own timeline. Then make a picture, if you like, of where you were and where you're going. It will remind you that everything changes.

Becoming a Master

A culture with a healthy respect for the experience of its elders is a culture of grace. A show of respect for a parent, teacher, mentor, sensei, guru, or master is appropriate as long as you don't relin-quish your own personal power in the process.

I've found that when students are out of balance, they either rebel against authority (certainly that was my way) or *fawn* over it, meaning they *court favor by excessive flattery, as courtiers will fawn over their king*—not a particularly healthy transaction for either person.

Then there is the student who fawns when around you but sharpens knives behind your back. They *want* your help but feel belittled when you give it. They accept help and punish you on their way out the door.

We live in such a competitive world; some students want to compete with the teacher. They want to challenge the "master" and show themselves off as better and brighter. They want to learn by challenging authority. They have paid the price of admission, not to study with you—but to posture to an attentive audience. I was like that. It's obnoxious. My teacher Milton was right—it's shitty.

It doesn't matter. None of these personality traits are important. We are all on our own path and will arrive at our destination in our own time. My dedication to teaching is simply the desire to shorten the arrival time a bit and encourage a healthy journey.

At best, the "unteachable student" serves as an example of how ego gets in the way of learning. *I want to do it myself* is the song of the insecure. We sometimes sell ourselves on the lie that *if someone helps me, my achievement doesn't count*.

Learning takes listening, and listening is a component of *being* present. It's an easy fix, really; we're just out of balance. We spend too much time *thinking* about ourselves and not enough time simply *being*, mostly because we don't know how. We are beings just learning how to BE.

We are never quite as brilliant as we *think* we are—nor as dreadful. We're always somewhere in between.

Forget comparing yourself to any master! Recognize that what you admire in that person is simply a reflection of those qualities already existent in *you*. Keep your eye on that ball. Therein lies the synchronicity: what you already knew, you summoned into your life for you to know *again*, more profoundly. Be grateful for that synchronicity.

Here's what I tell my students about *becoming a master*:

> *Start*
>
> *Keep going*
>
> *You think you're starting to get the hang of it*
>
> *Keep going*
>
> *You admire someone else's work and go into doubt, "Hell, I can't do that!"*
>
> *Keep going*
>
> *You feel like maybe...possibly...you've kind of got the hang of it now*
>
> *You don't*
>
> *Keep going*
>
> *You ask for someone's opinion—their response is insultingly polite*

Keep going

You fall into doubt

Keep going

You fall into depression

Keep going

You ask someone else's opinion—their response is favorable

You realize they have no idea what they're talking about

Keep going

You feel better and maybe even a little proud of what you can do now

Keep going

You chastise yourself for thinking that

Keep going

You indulge in some form of self-sabotage for comfort

Keep going

Self-loathing creeps in

Keep going

Depression visits...again

Keep going

You ask a professional for their opinion—they respond favorably

You think you know better

Keep going

You wake up sad

Keep going

Loneliness sets in

Keep going—although you can't possibly imagine why

You become restless

Keep going

You receive praise from the one person you believe matters most

It doesn't matter

Keep going...

You just keep going because there's nothing else you can do

Mastery arrives—you mistake it for a gust of wind

Keep going

You Are Enough

Actors strive to be "interesting." They're *thinking* all the time about how to be more marvelous. I love actors. I find them brave, soulful, and spirited. They are stunningly beautiful beings even when they try too hard at times.

"Here's the thing," I tell them. "You are enough. Don't add. Don't subtract. Just be."

> *YOU are unique*
>
> *There is no one like you*
>
> *We need your very distinct contribution in order to fulfill a harmony*
>
> *A vibration*
>
> *A universal chord*

Only when you settle into a relationship with yourself—heart over head—will you come into your own. Only then will you discover your own point of view.

Here is what my guides tell me and have asked me to pass on to you:

> *You are spectacular!*
>
> *You are more worthy, able, and divinely inspired than you can possibly imagine*
>
> *Bands of angels walk with you, encouraging you to stay the course*

256 • ARTIST

You are awakening

You are beloved

Breathe into your heart. Put an anchor there. Locate yourself, feet on Earth—and *look* at life from there. Head up. Heart full. Grateful.

Finding yourself in the quiet synergy of breath and heart is a way to locate *your soul.*

Now

The cat was howling his head off.

Come heeeeere! Come here NOOOW! We have always voiced our cats' thoughts for them.

NOW, DAD, NOW! I'm pretty sure you want to see this!

I listened as Miles got up from editing and schlepped into the kitchen, impatient and agitated. "What is it?!?" he yelled to Brody, our cat—one of three—beside himself with his find.

"WHOA!" Miles said when he arrived in the kitchen. "Okay, Brody—I see it! Oh, shit, hold on—HEY, JOCIE!" I heard him call out in alarm. "Can you come down here—NOW?"

I headed down the stairs as fast as I could. There at his feet, in the middle of the kitchen floor, was a beautiful lizard, with her tail whacked off at what looked like the midway point. "Oh! She's beautiful!" I said as I eyed the cat—proudly watching the scene unfold. "Where's her tail, little man?"

No answer from Brody.

The lizard, whom I named Zelda, was long—maybe four to five inches without her tail, green rather than brown, smooth as opposed to leathery, and on the fat side for a lizard.

I grabbed a cloth napkin off the counter and scooped her up. She squirmed only once before she stilled in my hand. I took her outside and put her in a giant pot of strawberry plants. She wriggled under their luscious green leaves—then poked her head up through some dead ones. She was perfectly disguised.

I thanked her for the visit and suggested this environment would be more to her liking. I saw her as a beautiful omen. Suddenly, a thought popped into my mind: I was serving Zelda in much the same way as my guides do *me*. I'd shifted her attention without her really knowing I was there. We were part of each other, a *whole,* if you will, even though we live in different dimensions.

Back inside, "the boys" (our three male cats and my husband) stood in a circle, still looking at the empty place where Zelda had been. They seemed a bit disappointed the excitement was over. I scanned the floor, looking for her tail.

We'd had a cat named Cagney when we lived in the Hollywood Hills who'd snapped many a lizard tail in his day. When I'd garden on weekends, he would bring me dozens of tailless lizards, and I'd pop them in a watering can and set them free at the end of the day. Saving lizards was nothing new to me.

"Oh, God!" I startled, making Miles jump a little.

"What?! WHAT?!" he said.

"There's her tail!" I whispered. It was on the other side of the room. I couldn't believe how long it was. It was another five inches, making her a good nine inches when she was whole. Oh, I wished I'd seen her whole!

I picked up her tail—I have to say, it's freaky to see their tails still moving after amputation. I took it back to Zelda. I placed it next to her in the strawberry pot and watched as it squirmed about—looking for her, no doubt.

I felt bad. Maybe it made her sad to see her tail like that, but I didn't know what else to do. I couldn't just throw it away when it still had so much life pulsing through it. Then again, it wasn't as if she could crawl over and magically reattach it, either. No, her tail would have to grow back, like all the other lizard tails.

As I watched her, she suddenly came to life and started to move toward the side of the pot, exploring the latitude of her new environment. At some point, she went up and over the lip, dove downward, and froze. Now, completely vertical—tail-stump to the sky, nose to the ground—she took on the new dimension, motionless. Time stood still, too. We breathed together.

Finally, she looked at me—CONTACT!

We took each other in.

Then, she looked away. My heart skipped a beat. *Wow, what a moment! Thank you.*

I stayed and watched until she made her way to the ground and scurried under the violets. "Goodbye, sweet creature—thank you for coming," I whispered. "I love you." No one could hear me but Zelda.

As I sat there, feeling blessed, I couldn't help but think about all the dimensions Zelda had just experienced—places that existed before she traveled to them and continued to exist after she was gone. There was the stone floor of the kitchen. The three giant cats and the man who called for help. There was an abduction and a blackout period as I carried her out of the kitchen in the napkin. There was the horizontal land of the strawberry pot—and the thirty-inch, vertical, clay-pot drop to cling to. And finally, the Earth, and plant life, and freedom to explore in a nourishing environment.

Observing Zelda's world made me think about how we were sharing the same space yet experiencing it in very different ways. It made me think of the other dimensions I sense around me—each existing as a parallel universe, whether you and I are aware of them or not.

Zelda had traveled through all kinds of places in the *now* and moved on—probably unaware that she was growing a new tail simply by *intending* balance.

It's well accepted that we learn by overcoming obstacles. It is less well understood that we create those obstacles ourselves as a direct reflection of our thoughts in the NOW.

What you do NOW determines everything that happens thereafter, just as it has always been. Just as it will always be. For *now*.

We simply need to understand we are *more* than these marvelous personalities we use as a means of identity. More than these fantastical bodies. More than our brilliant sensations. Much more. We are ambassadors of consciousness, each of us wrapped in our individual physical form. All of us are here in this brilliant dimension of time and space so that consciousness can reflect and experience itself as life.

My journey has been about discovering myself as a presence in this spirited moment of NOW. I have done so through the study, practice, and instruction of acting. My intention has been to help people create more artistry and joy in their lives. I want to help people make conscious choices that contribute in a positive manner.

Along with exercises and techniques, I recommend meditation practice as a way of accessing inspiration from your higher self for both life and work.

Once you locate yourself in the stillness, once you turn from head to heart, from ego to soul, once you find yourself in the present moment—that pure white canvas of consciousness where *all* possibility exists—you begin to manifest the life of your dreams. You begin to contribute to the whole of humankind in the way your higher self intends.

It's time to recognize and accept our true nature. It's time to wake up to the possibilities of what we can consciously create with our life. It's time to embrace the highest version of ourselves by *practicing* basic integrities like kindness, honesty, and doing the right thing for ourselves and others.

We were made for these times. We came here to be a part of this great shift. We are ready.

The time is NOW!

Metta Meditation:
Cultivating Joy for Yourself and Others

If I could have but one prayer in life, it would be a prayer of gratitude. If I could have but one meditation, it would be offering Metta.

Metta (*Maitri* in Sanskrit) means loving-kindness, goodwill, benevolence, amity, and a healthy interest in others. It is the first of the four sublime states in the traditional Buddhist practice. The goal of Metta meditation is to cultivate kindness and compassion for yourself and all beings. You don't have to be a Buddhist to practice loving-kindness, and I can think of nothing we need more in the world right now than offering Metta to ourselves and others.

To practice loving-kindness, sit upright in a relaxed manner. Your tailbone moves toward the Earth, the crown of your head toward the Heavens. Let go of any concerns or preoccupations by listening to your breath. Take slow, deep inhalations and long, complete exhalations. Open your heart. Let your feelings of goodwill expand outward with each breath.

Since we have difficulty loving others without first loving ourselves, we first direct Metta toward *self*. As you sit and breathe, slowly repeat the following phrases in your mind. While you say these phrases, allow their intentions to fill you. Take your time.

May I be safe

May I be healthy

May I be happy

May I be free

After directing loving-kindness toward yourself for a time, think of someone you love. Then, slowly repeat phrases of loving-kindness while holding their image in your mind.

May you be safe

May you be healthy

May you be happy

May you be free

After a while, if you wish, bring a *neutral* person to mind—a neighbor or the mail carrier.

May you be safe

May you be healthy

May you be happy

May you be free

If you like, you can work with a person you have difficulty with. If, during the meditation, seemingly opposite feelings arise—such as anger, grief, or sadness—take these feelings as a sign that you are opening up. You may want to shift to simply observing your feelings with compassion, experiencing them, and letting them go. Or you can continue to offer Metta to this person with whatever patience, acceptance, and equanimity you can.

Above all, remember that there is no need to judge yourself for having feelings. Hold the person in your heart, and direct the loving-kindness phrases to them.

May you be safe

May you be healthy

May you be happy

May you be free

And finally, you can direct loving-kindness to all beings.

May all *beings be safe*

May all *beings be healthy*

May all *beings be happy*

May all *beings be free*

If you research Metta, you will find many different phrases that serve the intentions of this meditation. I encourage you to create your own variation of these phrases. My favorite is:

Inhale: May I be safe,

Exhale: Safe from all inner and outer harm.

Inhale: May I be healthy,

Exhale: Healthy in both body and mind.

Inhale: May I be happy,

Exhale: And filled with the joy of a grateful heart.

Inhale: May I be free,

Exhale: And live my life in peace.

Loving-kindness meditation is a way to bless the self and others with peace and happiness. It is a profound way to begin and end the day. Metta meditation is a healing.

From my heart to yours:

May you be safe

May you be healthy

May you be happy

May you be free

Acknowledgments

FIRST AND FOREMOST, I AM ETERNALLY GRATEFUL FOR MY HUSBAND Miles, who read every draft as if it were the first and, knowing me as he does, gave me the clearest editorial notes anyone could wish for. Without his love, there would be no memoir. Miles has always focused his light on the best in me. He inspired me to practice living without judgment. He has taught me what it is to be a good partner and parent. And when my behavior slipped to rude, inappropriate, or conduct well beneath me, I would hear him whisper lovingly, *Darlin', it doesn't become you.* Miles has taught me what it is to love and be loved unconditionally.

Then there is the rest of the tribe I am blessed to have walked beside on this grand journey. They encouraged me to stay the course, inspired me with their notes, and affirmed that my efforts merited persistence. Without this intimate community of readers, the book wouldn't be what it is today. Thank you from the bottom of my heart for reading every word and cheering me along the way: Samantha Watkins, Matthew Berkowitz, Leah Remini, Rachel Simon, Liza Macrae, Bobby Field, Penny Fuller, Kelly Rutherford, Lana Parrilla, Michael Pressman, David Knoller, David Jones, Mimi Maynard, Jennifer Gelfer, Ileane Meltzer, and Lilly Holden.

I'd also like to thank David Englander, Marjorie Galen, Mary Ellen Ledwith, Susan Nemesdy, Nadine Campbell, Sandra Duncan, and

Elizabeth Forbes for supporting me in the darkest days of "Living with Dying." Every one of these people went out of their way and offered a quality of kindness that provided, in many ways, the beginning inspirations for this book.

Special thanks to the Story Summit for acknowledging an early draft of *Artist* with a Best Memoir award and for inviting me into an extraordinary community of teachers and writers, including Debra Engle, an editor who reminded me early on to trust in the power of my own inner guidance and stay positive with the work.

A very special thanks to my mentor David Paul Kirkpatrick, who read the book with enthusiasm, gifted me with his wisdom, and encouraged me in ways that elevated my confidence. David serves as my definition of friendship and generosity.

Special thanks to Jenny Shipley, the editor who shaped the book and made it flow in ways I never imagined. To Erin Michelle Sky, for her heartfelt copy. To Rebecca Lown, for her beautiful cover art. And to Aleza D'Agostino for her infectiously positive attitude.

I'd like to thank *all* my teachers, good and bad, as the lessons learned were the lessons needed. Most especially, I'd like to thank Irene Dirmann and Milton Katselas, who served as the yin and yang of my education as both teacher and student.

And with all my heart, I'd like to thank my students, who taught me every bit as much as I might have imparted. My heart grew in leaps and bounds due to your presence in my life. I love you all.

Lastly, I give thanks every day for the inner guidance I've been blessed with. Much of this book has been channeled. How much, I couldn't say. That line has blurred—as it will for all of us, eventually.

About the Author

Jocelyn Jones has been an acting teacher for over thirty years. From A-list movie stars to hand-picked beginners, Ms. Jones is known for offering insights and techniques that enhance her clients' confidence; provide consistent, inspirational results; and guide them to their own unique perspectives. Her memoir is a blueprint for awakening and connecting to the spirit within—the artist, capable of manifesting anything.

Ms. Jones is also known for the critically acclaimed documentary series *In Class with Jocelyn Jones: A Celebration of Actors & Acting*, featuring sixteen studio members as they demonstrate the range of work taught in her Master Class. Learn more at JocelynJonesStudio.com.

CPSIA information can be obtained
at www.ICGtesting.com
Printed in the USA
LVHW051308030322
712397LV00008B/787